COMING TO AMERICA

The East Indians

Other books in the Coming to America series:

COMING TO
AMERICA

The East Indians

Adriane Ruggiero, Book Editor

GREENHAVEN PRESS
An imprint of Thomson Gale, a part of The Thomson Corporation

Detroit • New York • San Francisco • New Haven, Conn. • Waterville, Maine • London

Christine Nasso, *Publisher*
Elizabeth Des Chenes, *Managing Editor*

© 2006 Thomson Gale, a part of The Thomson Corporation.

Thomson and Star logo are trademarks and Gale and Greenhaven Press are registered trademarks used herein under license.

For more information, contact:
Greenhaven Press
27500 Drake Rd.
Farmington Hills, MI 48331-3535
Or you can visit our Internet site at http://www.gale.com

LIBRARY OF CONGRESS CATALOGING-IN-PUBLICATION DATA

The East Indians / Adriane Ruggiero, book editor.
    p. cm. -- (Coming to America)
    Includes bibliographical references and index.
    ISBN-13: 978-0-7377-3498-0 (hardcover : alk. paper)
    ISBN-10: 0-7377-3498-1 (hardcover : alk. paper)
    1. East Indian Americans--History--Juvenile literature. 2. East Indian Americans--Social conditions--Juvenile literature. 3. Immigrants--United States--History--Juvenile literature. 4. India--Emigration and immigration--History--Juvenile literature. 5. United States--Emigration and immigration--History--Juvenile literature. I. Ruggiero, Adriane.
    E184.E2E18 2007
    973'.04914--dc22
                                                    2006022918

Printed in the United States of America
10 9 8 7 6 5 4 3 2 1

Contents

Chapter 2: The Second Wave of East Indian Immigrants

Chapter 3: A Third and Continuing Wave: Accomplishments and Challenges

Samina Ali, a Muslim Indian writer who has lived in the United States since the age of eight, has written novels about the experiences of Muslims in the United States and India.

Foreword

In her popular novels, such as *The Joy Luck Club* and *The Bonesetter's Daughter*, Chinese American author Amy Tan explores the complicated cultural and social differences between Chinese-born mothers and their American-born daughters. For example, the mothers eat foods and hold religious beliefs that their daughters either abhor or abstain from, while the daughters pursue educational and career opportunities that were not available to the previous generation. Generation gaps occur in almost all families, but as Tan's writings show, such differences are even more pronounced when parents grow up in a different country. When immigrants come to the United States, their initial goal is often to start a new life that is an improvement from the life they experienced in their homeland. However, while these newcomers may intend to fully adapt to American culture, they inevitably bring native customs with them. Immigrants have helped make America broader culturally by introducing new religions, languages, foods, and different ways of looking at the world. Their children and subsequent generations, however, often seek to cast aside these traditions and instead more fully absorb mainstream American mores.

As Tan's writings suggest, the dissimilarities between immigrants and their children are manifested in several ways. Adults who come to the United States and do not learn English turn to their children, educated in the American school system, to serve as interpreters and translators. Children, seeing what their American-born schoolmates eat, reject the foods of their native land. Religion is another area where the generation gap is particularly pronounced. For example, the liturgy of Syrian Christian services had to be translated into English when most young Syrian Americans no longer knew how to speak Syriac. Numerous Jews, freed from the European ghettos they had lived in, wished to assimilate more fully into the surrounding culture and began to loosen the traditional dietary and ritual requirements under which they had grown up. Reformed Judaism, which began in Germany, thus found a strong foothold among young Jews born in America.

However, no generational experiences have been as significant as that between immigrant mothers and their daughters. Living in the United States has afforded girls and young women opportunities they likely would not have had in their homelands. The daughters of immigrants, in some cases, live entirely different lives than their mothers did in their native nations. Where an Arab mother may have only received a limited education, her American-raised daughter enjoys a full course of American public schooling, often continuing on to college and careers. A woman raised in India might have been placed in an arranged marriage, while her daughter will have the opportunity to date and choose a husband. Admittedly, not all families have been willing to give their daughters all these new freedoms, but these American-born girls are frequently more willing to declare their wishes.

The generation gap is only one aspect of the immigrant experience in the United States. Understanding immigrants' unique and shared experiences and their contributions to American life is an interesting way to study the many people who make up the American citizenry. Greenhaven Press's Coming to America series helps readers learn why more people have moved to the United States than to any other nation. Selections on the lives of immigrants once they have reached America, from their struggles to find employment to their experiences with discrimination and prejudice, help give students insights into stereotypes and cultural mores that continue to this day. Finally, profiles of prominent immigrants help the reader become aware of the many achievements of these people in fields ranging from science to politics to sports.

Each volume in the Coming to America series takes an extensive look into a particular immigrant population. The carefully selected primary and secondary sources provide both historical perspectives and firsthand insights into the immigrant experience. Combined with an in-depth introduction and a comprehensive chronology and bibliography, every book in the series is a valuable addition to the study of American history. With immigrants comprising nearly 12 percent of the U.S. population, and their children and grandchildren constantly adding to the population, the immigrant experience continues to evolve. Coming to America is consequently a beneficial tool for not only understanding America's past but also its future.

Introduction

East Indians are among the fastest growing immigrant groups in the United States representing 1.7 million persons. They come from every state in India as well as from England, Canada, South Africa, Tanzania, Fiji, Guyana, and Trinidad—places where Indians and their fellow South Asians migrated to over the decades. They are spread out across the nation and live in cities as diverse as New York, Chicago, Houston, and Los Angeles. They also live in suburbs of the major metropolitan areas. East Indians also belong to many religious faiths, including Hinduism, Islam, Sikhism, Jainism, Christianity, and Zoroastrianism. Many East Indian immigrants have high professional skills and are doctors, scientists, technologists, and engineers. They are also filmmakers, writers, musicians, and heads of corporations. Because of India's history as a possession of Great Britain, East Indians speak English and are familiar with Western culture. These factors have been advantages to them as immigrants to the United States.

East Indian Immigrants Then and Now

East Indian immigration is a relatively recent phenomenon in the United States dating as it does from the mid-1960s. Before that time, East Indians were a small immigrant group subsumed within the category of "Asian" by ignorant American immigration officials. Government policies and societal attitudes have changed with the passage of time and today East Indians are a distinctive ethnic group in the United States as are their fellow South Asians: Pakistanis, Bangladeshis, and Sri Lankans. The East Indians have come a long way since the days of the poor and illiterate East Indian immigrants of the late 1800s and early 1900s. That generation of immigrants were laborers fleeing poverty and deprivation in their homeland. In America, they were allowed to work when and where their labor was needed but were often attacked for their skin color and ethnicity when American workers felt their jobs threatened. In addition, they were denied the right to become citizens.

Today, East Indian immigrants are more likely to be educated and middle- and upper-class. They make up one of the richest ethnic groups in America. During the technology boom of the late 1990s, Indian entrepreneurs and technologists who were trained in India and the United States were responsible for 10 percent of the start-up companies in California's Silicon Valley. Their skills, energy, and willingness to take risks led to innovations in computing and global communications. The East Indian immigrants of recent years have taken full advantage of their rights as citizens. They are unafraid of speaking out when they believe they are being discriminated against in the workplace, the community, or elsewhere. They have also embraced the responsibilities of being citizens by taking part in politics and seeking elective office. As lawmakers they represent everyone in their constituencies but also draw national attention to East Indian culture and contributions to the United States. This is a recent development for an immigrant group that often seemed more interested in their economic and cultural achievements.

The Struggle for Civil Rights

The East Indian immigrants of the early 1900s were primarily agricultural workers who wanted to buy farm land in the United States. However, the laws of the time forbade East Indians to become citizens and to buy land. The laws were particularly stringent on the west coast of the United States where most of the East Indian immigrants were located. In 1913, the state of California enacted the Alien Land Law. This legislation restricted the ability to sell or lease land to persons ineligible for citizenship. East Indians were part of this ineligible group. Some immigrants found a way around the law by marrying Mexican Americans and melding into that ethnic group. Others left the United States for good. Political events in India also influenced the drive for East Indian rights in America. Founded by East Indian students in San Francisco in 1913, the Ghadar movement aimed to rally Indians in the United States and other countries to fight for Indian independence from Great Britain. One result of the movement was to stir East Indian activists in the United States to demand citizenship for themselves. However, World War I and the 1920s saw setbacks to the East Indian fight for civil rights. The United States and Great Britain were allies and U.S. policies supported those of Great Britain and not those of Indian freedom fighters. Racist attiudes toward East Indians continued. In a 1923 decision the Supreme Court ruled that an East Indian by the name of Bhagat Singh Thind could not become a citizen on the grounds that he was not Caucasian in the common person's understanding of the term. The Thind decision also provided a way for the government to annul all previous Indian naturalizations and subjected Indian landowners to the California Alien Land Law.

The *Thind* decision was another blow to East Indian demands for citizenship. Already shrinking in population on account of the land laws, many East Indians left the United States and moved elsewhere. But those who remained continued to lobby for citizenship during the 1930s and 1940s. They were inspired by the activities of Mahatma Gandhi on behalf of Indian independence from Great Britain. They also argued that India's role as an outpost of resistance to Japanese aggression and expansionism in Asia was proof that East Indians should be granted the right of citizenship in the United States. After 1943, when barriers to Chinese immigration and naturalization were done away with, East Indians began to demand the same rights as the Chinese. In Washington, D.C., political activists such as Arizona farmer Mubarak Ali Khan, founder of the Indian Welfare League, worked to help sway American opinion on behalf of Indian citizenship. Another activist, New York businessman Sardar Jagjit Singh, helped found the India League of America in 1938 and used his political and business connections to cast a spotlight on India and East Indians. He arranged for congresswoman Clare Booth Luce to visit India and convinced *Time* magazine to publish stories in support of Indian independence. Their efforts paid off.

After World War II and the passage of the Luce-Celler Act in 1946, East Indians were allowed to become naturalized citizens. Those who had been denied citizenship after decades of living in the United States were now able to become naturalized. East Indians were also given a quota for immigration. As a result, many East Indian men who had families in India were able to bring their wives, children, and other relatives to the United States. The influx of East Indians to the United States was not great at first but grew during the 1950s.

Growing Visibility Leads to a Greater Political Voice

East Indians gained more visibility in the United States in the post-World War II era but were not really well known in a national sense. This changed in 1956 when a one-time lettuce farmer from California's Imperial Valley, Dalip Singh Saund, ran for Congress and won. He was the first East Indian to be elected to Congress. Despite his presence as a political figure, many East Indians did not follow Dalip Singh Saund into politics. Greater involvement would have to wait until another wave of immigration took place.

East Indian immigrants came to the United States in record numbers after the 1965 Immigration Act established a nonnational system of preferences and opened the nation's doors to immigrants from Latin America, Asia, Africa, and the Caribbean. Like so many immigrant groups before them, the East Indian immigrants of this era were seeking better-paying jobs, opportunities for advanced education, and a new life for themselves and their children. Yet many of the East Indian immigrants of the 1960s through the 1980s planned to return to India once they had achieved their goals. Still tied to family and culture in India they saw America as a temporary stopping place. This fact lessened their inclination to assimilate into American society. Nevertheless, economic opportunities in America, the openness of its society, and the educational possibilities available for their children convinced many to make their permanent homes in the United States.

The existence of vibrant East Indian communities in the major cities and some suburbs of America helped many immigrants ease the transition from homeland to adopted land. These "Little Indias" with their grocery stores, travel agencies, restaurants, and newspapers also made it possible for newcomers to retain cultural ties to India and soften the sense of separation. In addition, the immigrants of the 1960s who were professionals were quick to establish professional organizations, community newsletters, and political and economic coalitions for communicating their concerns and issues both to other East Indians and to the larger American society. One of the concerns was the rise of hate crimes against East Indians in the aftermath of the terrorist attacks of September 11, 2001. Sikhs were a particular target on account of their beards and turbans. During this time of fear and rage, East Indians spoke out against incidences of racism and zenophobia they encountered in their workplaces, schools, and neighborhoods.

Opening Lines of Communication

The lines of global communication have grown tremendously with the rise of the Internet in the late 1990s. Today, there are numerous Web sites (with new ones appearing every day) devoted to nearly every aspect of Indian American life. These sites serve as outlets for Indian Americans to communicate their concerns, ideas, and issues to their fellow East Indians and also to anyone interested in reading and learning about them. One of the leading sites is India Abroad Center for Political Awareness, based in Washington, D.C. This organization's goal is to disseminate information about Indian Americans in the United States and advocate Indian participation in the political system. Its newsletter, the National Wire, reaches over 1,500 people on a quarterly basis.

For the most part East Indians of the post-1965 era have achieved a better economic life than the one they had in India. Their rise in economic standing has translated into home ownership and college degrees for their children. Middle class as the result of their work ethic, the older generation has high expectations for their children and has instilled in them the belief in hard work and excellence. It is no surprise then that many young Indian Americans have become doctors, scientists, technologists, and entrepreneurs. The young generation of Indian Americans are proud of their rich culture and of their parents' sacrifices but are interested in forming identities that have less to do with India and more to do with being American. Unlike their parents, who may have been reticent about their immigrant background, Indian American youth are generally at ease in an ethnically and racially diverse United States. They are deeply interested in communicating their feelings about being Indian and American.

A Strong Voice Getting Stronger

Many Indian American youths feel the sting of racism on account of the way they dress, how they decorate themselves, or the color of their skin. And they also feel they are too often stereotyped as subservient women, or as techno geeks, math prodigies, or yogis. They believe it is their duty to fight racism and dispel mistaken notions about Indian Americans. One way to do this is to take part in politics. The election of November 2002 proved a point in showing Indian Americans' commitment to political life. In that election year twenty-five

East Indians ran for elective office on the Democratic, Republican, and Green party tickets. Five were successful in their attempts. In Maryland, Kumar Barve won a fourth term to the Maryland House of Delegates and in Minnesota Satveer Chaudhary retained his seat in the Minnesota State Senate. Two years later, Louisiana native Bobby Jindal was elected to Congress. Jindal fits the model of an excelling young Indian American: Rhodes scholar and graduate of Oxford University, former president of the Louisiana University System, and Assistant Secretary for Planning and Evaluation in the Department of Health and Human Services. In 2006 Jindal was involved with other Louisiana government leaders in helping guide federal monies to areas of the state destroyed by Hurricane Katrina.

Today, many Indian Americans have achieved wealth and status in America. The young generation believed that it is time to focus on other areas of their lives, such as government service. By serving as interns in Congressional offices, running campaigns for their candidates, and conducting leadership workshops for fellow students they hope to raise Indian American awareness of the political system of which they are a part.

COMING TO
AMERICA

CHAPTER 1

The First East Indian Immigrants

Punjabi Immigrants of the Early 1900s

Padma Rangaswamy

In this selection Padma Rangaswamy traces the history of East Indians in America from the arrival of poor farmers from the Indian state of Punjab in the early 1900s to the immigration of the 1930s, when better-educated Indians came to the United States.

Rangaswamy also explains some of the reasons East Indian immigrants became the target of white, nativist discrimination that culminated in anti-immigration laws. As the author points out, however, the poor and illiterate East Indian immigrants in the early wave were not completely powerless against discriminatory laws and practices. They found ways around the laws that allowed them to keep their landholdings in their families, for example. Better-educated immigrants took the battle for citizenship rights directly to the courts and won in several landmark cases. Despite setbacks to their struggle for full equality, this group of intellectuals became the leaders of the next generation of East Indian immigrants who, in their turn, ushered in an era of full political participation.

Rangaswamy is project coordinator for the Neigborhood History Project at the Chicago Historical Society. She researched the East Indian community in Chicago for her book Namasté America. *Namasté is a Sanskrit word meaning "I bow before you." It is a common Indian greeting.*

The first Indian in the United States is said to have been a man from Madras who visited Salem, Massachusetts, in 1790 with a sea captain, according to an entry in an

Padma Rangaswamy, *Namaste America: Indian Immigrants in an American Metropolis.* University Park: Pennsylvania State University Press, 2000, pp. 41–45. Copyright © 2000 by the Pennsylvania State University. All rights reserved. Reproduced by permission of the Pennsylvania State University Press.

eighteenth-century diary, but there is no way of determining the accuracy of this report. During the nineteenth century, there were a few scattered adventurers, merchants, and seafarers who paid sporadic visits to New York and San Francisco. The records of the Immigration and Naturalization Service show a solitary Indian admitted to the United States in 1820 and a total of 716 arrivals from 1820 to 1900. One of India's leading spiritual luminaries came as early as 1893 to Chicago and introduced his message of the universal philosophy of Vedanta to the West. Swami Vivekananda came to the World Columbian Exposition and delivered his famous, electrifying speech to the World's Parliament of Religions in what is now the Art Institute of Chicago. Though Swami Vivekananda visited Chicago frequently in later years, his visits didn't lead to any permanent Indian presence in the United States until the Vedanta Society of Chicago was established in 1930. Among these early Indians, there were also a few students and political refugees who fled to North America to escape the wrath of the British. The 1900 Census of the United States counted 2,050 Indians, but one cannot be sure how many of these were temporary visitors—or even if they were truly Indian—because the records were based on place of birth rather than race or ethnicity.

The First Wave of Indian Immigrants

It was not until the turn of the century that the first significant wave of immigrants from India landed on the shores of North America. Most of the seven thousand or so Indians who came to the United States between the years 1904 and 1920 were not indentured labor; still, as illiterate peasants from Punjab, their experiences were very different from the experiences of the Chicago Indians of the post-1965 migration. It is important to briefly recount their history as part of the Indian immigrant legacy in the United States. Some of the themes that are relevant to both periods of immigration include the immigrants' origin in India and how it influenced their work and lifestyle in the United States, what tactics they used to struggle against the policies of the American government and white society; and how their identity as Indians in the United States was affected by their involvement with their homeland. Despite the obvious differences and contrasts, some important similarities also come to light when the "old" immigration is considered in the light of the "new."

In the late 1890s, farming in the Punjab became difficult as drought and famine took their toll, and changes in the British land-tenure system put the small landowner in a vulnerable situation. At about this time, Canadian steamship companies, acting on behalf of Pacific coast employers who were looking for cheap labor in their lumber mills, visited the villages of Punjab and distributed pamphlets, touting the economic opportunities in British Columbia. Lured by such promise, thousands of villagers left Punjab, in search of fortune. At first they came as sojourners hoping to make money in a short while and return to their families, so most came without their wives. They landed in British Columbia, in an environment already inflamed by white hatred for the Chinese and Japanese who had arrived before them in large numbers. Forced by racist attacks to flee Canada, the Sikhs [followers of Sikhism, a religion that arose in the Punjab] made their way southward down the Pacific coast, working in the lumber mills of Bellingham and Everett in Washington state and then on railroad construction and maintenance crews, until they reached the warmer climes of California. Between 1907 and 1908, the Southern Pacific Railroad, the Northern Electric Company Railroad, and the Western Pacific Railroad employed between fifteen hundred and two thousand Indians. The Sikhs remained culturally apart, and kept to themselves, cooking their own food in crowded camps on the outskirts of town. Their lifestyle was governed largely by the fact that there were few women in the group. Less than 10 percent of the single men married while in the United States. Organized white groups, suspicious of the alien culture and resentful of the cheap labor provided by the hardworking Sikhs, launched violent attacks against them and ran a successful campaign to bar their entry to the United States. Their efforts resulted in the Barred Zone Act of 1917, which effectively cut off all immigration from India.

After the railroads were built, the Indians [in California] went to work in the Chico sugar beet farms, the fruit orchards near Sacramento, the vineyards of Fresno, and the San Joaquin delta near Stockton. They quickly rose from merely laboring in the farms to leasing and purchasing land, pooling their resources, and investing collectively. Many of them attained economic prosperity, developing the arid lands into profitable rice fields and becoming known locally as the "Hindu rice kings." By 1930, Indians in the United States were mostly Pacific coast farmers, numbering roughly three thousand. There were another one thousand skilled workers, merchants, and traders in the eastern United States. Others in the Indian immigrant category included about five hundred students scattered throughout the United States, and twenty-five to thirty Swamis, or holy men. Immigration remained static throughout the 1930s and until the end of World War II.

The Struggle Against Discrimination

In the general atmosphere of hostility toward them in the United States, Indians kept nationalist sentiments alive and invested much of their energies in revolutionary activities designed to win freedom for India from the British. Intellectuals and farmers alike came together to form the *Ghadr* party (*Ghadr* meaning "revolution" in Arabic). Activists such as Taraknath Das and Har Daval published newspapers and founded societies to attract Americans to the cause. At first, they believed the United States would be a haven for revolutionaries, but they were soon disillusioned. A group of Indians set sail from San Francisco to Calcutta in 1914 with the express purpose of fomenting an uprising in the Punjab, but the leaders were arrested in India and the movement quickly collapsed.

For a long time, historians portrayed the illiterate farmers from Punjab as helpless in the face of the anti-Asian laws that openly discriminated against them. It was believed that if there was any struggle on the part of the Indians for their rights, it came only from the educated elite of students and businessmen. But recent scholarship shows how the struggle for individual rights against both the government and white society was actually carried out on two fronts, by the illiterate farmers in their own and no less effective way than by the educated, well-to-do Indians in the legal arena. Antimiscegenation laws in California prevented the unskilled farmers and laborers in the West from marrying white women. So many of them married Mexican women and raised families of Punjabi-Mexican identity. The intellectuals in the eastern universities chose to marry white women, but they, too, had to face discriminatory laws and fight for their civil rights in court.

The Alien Land Acts[1] of California, first enacted in 1913 and strengthened in later years, were primarily aimed against the Japanese and Chinese, but they also prevented the Sikhs from owning land. Sikhs got around the system by using whatever legal and economic means they could to set up elaborate and complicated partnerships, at first with Anglos [whites] and later on with their own minor children who had citizenship rights, so they would always be able to control the land that they worked on.

Fighting for Civil Rights in the Courts

While the farmers worked around the system to get the better of it, the intellectuals fought head-on to change the system in the courts. In see-saw battles, the Indians learned that the

---

1. Laws that made it impossible for those aliens ineligible for citizenship to own agricultural property. Japanese, Chinese, and East Indians were aliens ineligible for citizenship.

judges provided their own free-wheeling interpretation of what constituted "white" and "Caucasian" and sometimes formulated opinions only to suit the public mood. The 1790 federal law that reserved citizenship for "whites only" effectively prohibited Asians from getting citizenship, but in landmark court cases such as *United States v. Balsara* (1910) and *[United States v.] A. Kumar Mazumdar* (1913), Indians were declared eligible for citizenship by the Supreme Court because they were "Caucasian" like the Europeans. About one hundred Indians were naturalized between 1913 and 1923. Then, in a dramatic reversal, in the *Bhagat Singh Thind* case in 1923, Justice George Sutherland ruled that being "Caucasian" was not enough to be considered "white" and Indians were not "free white persons" and therefore were ineligible for citizenship. Following this ruling, the U.S. government revoked the citizenship of some fifty Indians until Dr. Sakharam Ganesh Pandit, a lawyer himself and married to a white American, fought denaturalization proceedings successfully, and in 1927 won the right to retain his citizenship. While this case stopped the government from taking away the citizenship of those already naturalized, no further naturalizations were permitted. Aware that they were unwelcome in the United States, some three thousand Indians left for India between 1920 and 1940. Many Indians who had their citizenship revoked found themselves in dire straits, stripped of their property in the United States, their bridges to India burned. One such immigrant, Vaisho Das Bagai, even took his life in despair. The return migration was large enough to render questionable the idea of immigration as a one-way stream. . . .

One dramatic example of an individual who took full advantage of the rights of citizenship is Dalip Singh Saund. He was elected a member of the Eighty-fifth Congress from the Imperial and Riverside counties of California and served three terms from 1957 to 1963. He also served on the House Foreign Relations Committee. . . . Saund, who earned a doctorate from the University of California, personally explained the effects of earlier discriminatory laws. "Few opportunities existed for me or people of my nationality in the state at the time. I was not a citizen and could not become one. The only way Indians in California could make a living . . . was to join with others who had settled in various parts of the state as farmers." In the 1940s, the Punjabi immigrants of the early twentieth century were an all but forgotten group. Their numbers had dwindled to a mere fifteen hundred by 1946. What prevented the Sikhs from either upholding their distinct culture in the United States or entering the mainstream were their small numbers and their illiteracy. By contrast, similar illiterate and disadvantaged Indians who went as indentured labor to the East [Coast] and West Indies in the mid-nineteenth century did manage to retain a distinct identity but their numbers were much larger. Lack of formal education and low economic status have generally contributed to culture dilution among Indians. It is the upper-class elite who have functioned as the torchbearers among newer Indian immigrant groups and set the tone for the post-1965 immigration to the industrialized countries of Great Britain, the United States, Canada, and Australia. In 1946, the Luce-Celler Bill granted, among other things, citizenship rights to Indians and allotted India a quota of one hundred immigrants per annum [year]. A gradual trickle of legal immigration began and continued through the 1950s and 1960s.

East Indian Immigrants Face Discrimination in America

Ronald Takaki

As writer Ronald Takaki points out in the following selection, the East Indian immigrants who arrived in the United States in the early years of the twentieth century faced numerous obstacles, including the racism and xenophobia of white Americans. As Takaki notes, some white Americans considered the dark-skinned East Indians as blacks and treated them with disdain. Other Americans mistakenly grouped all East Indians under the name of "Hindoo" regardless of whether they were Hindu, Muslim, or Sikh.

Takaki also describes the life of East Indians on the West Coast of the United States, where they were often subject to violent attacks. These attacks were led by American workers who feared the loss of jobs to the immigrants. The racial fears were stoked by the Asian Exclusion League, a San Francisco–based organization that opposed Asian immigration to the United States. The fact that the Indians worked at the least desirable jobs for long hours and low wages did nothing to lessen the hatred white Americans felt toward them, Takaki writes.

Takaki is professor of ethnic studies at the University of California at Berkeley. His other works include Iron Cages: Race and Culture in Nineteenth-Century America *and* A Different Mirror: A History of Multicultural America.

In 1865, the Hawaiian Board of Immigration sent labor agent William Hillebrand to China to recruit laborers, instructing him to proceed from China to the East Indies to investigate the possibility of India as a labor source. Hillebrand

Ronald Takaki, *Strangers from a Different Shore: A History of Asian Americans*. Boston: Little Brown, 1989, pp. 294–97, 301–4. Copyright © 1989, 1998 by Ronald Takaki. Reproduced by permission of Little, Brown, and Co., Inc. In the rest of the world by permission of the author.

was not able to complete his mission, but Hawaiian planters continued to cultivate an interest in procuring laborers from India. "Where shall we look for the kind of immigrants we need to supply us with both a homogeneous population and labor?" asked the *Pacific Commercial Advertiser* in 1874. "We answer, to the East Indies. From the teeming millions of Bengal and other provinces of Hindostan." Seven years later, planters appealed to the Hawaiian Minister of Foreign Affairs for his "assistance in removing the obstacles in the way of introducing East Indian Coolies into these islands." In 1884, when they learned that Japan had decided to permit emigration to the islands, the planters turned away from India for their labor needs.

Twenty years later, Asian Indians suddenly began appearing in the lumber towns of Washington and the agricultural fields of California. By 1920, some sixty-four hundred had entered the United States. Many of them had carried "extravagant" dreams to America, but all became "strangers," driven by a new "necessity" here. Like the Koreans, they did not develop a colony or distinct ethnic community with geographical boundaries. A small and somewhat dispersed group, they did not form an Indiatown. Theirs is an especially interesting and important story. Asian Indians represented a new diversity in the Asian migrations east to America. Though they were, like their Asian brethren, "strangers from a different shore," they were Caucasian. . . .

Exotic Hindus

Called "Hindus" in America, only a small fraction of the Asian-Indian immigrants were actually believers of Hinduism. One third were Muslim, and the majority were Sikhs. As believers of Sikhism, they were required to wear the "five *k*'s"—*kes* (unshorn hair and beard), *kacch* (trousers to the knee), *kara* (iron bangle), *kirpan* (sword) or *khanda* (dagger), *khanga* (hair comb).

Wearing their traditional headdress, the newcomers from India were described as "the tide of turbans." "Always the turban remains," a witness wrote, "the badge and symbol of their native land, their native customs and religion. Whether repairing tracks on the long stretches of the Northern Pacific railways, feeding logs into the screaming rotary saws of the lumber-mills, picking fruit in the luxuriant orchards or sunny hillsides of California, the twisted turban shows white or brilliant . . . an exotic thing in the western landscape." Their different dress and their dark skin provoked taunts and verbal abuse from whites. "I used to go to Marysville every Saturday," recounted a Sikh [quoted by state historian H.A. Millis]. "One day a drunk *ghora* (white man) came out of a bar and motioned to me saying, 'Come here, slave!' I said I was no slave man. He told me that his race ruled India and America, too. All we were slaves. He came close to me and I hit him and got away fast."

While Asian-Indian immigrants found themselves called "niggers," they were more frequently associated with the Chinese and Japanese. "Sixty years' contact with the Chinese, and twenty-five years' experience with the Japanese and two or three years' acquaintance with Hindus," declared American Federation of Labor president Samuel Gompers in 1908, "should be sufficient to convince any ordinarily intelligent person that they have no standards . . . by which a Caucasian may judge them." The Asiatic Exclusion League agreed, blaming the Japanese and the Asian Indians for the violence directed against them: "In California the insolence and presumption of Japanese, and the immodest and filthy habits of the Hindoos are continually involving them in trouble, beatings. . . . In all these cases, we may say the Oriental is at fault." In 1910 *Collier's Weekly* claimed that the immigrants from India were "inferior workmen," differing from "the unobtrusive Chinaman by being sullen and uncompromising" [according to historian Joan M. Jensen]. . . .

Labor Troubles and Exclusion

Asian Indians were especially feared as labor competitors by white workers and were often victimized by white working-class antagonism and violence. In September 1907, several hundred white workers invaded the Asian-Indian community in Bellingham, Washington, and drove seven hundred Asian Indians across the border into Canada. Two months later, white workers forcibly rounded up Asian Indians in Everett and expelled them from the town. In San Francisco, the Asiatic Exclusion League issued warnings of the new "menace" from India. Addressing the "Hindoo question," the league denounced the immigrants as competitors of white labor and as dirty, lustful, and diseased. "From every part of the Coast," the league claimed, "complaints are made of the undesirability of the Hindoos, their lack of cleanliness, disregard of sanitary laws, petty pilfering, especially of chickens, and insolence to women."

In response to exclusionist pressures, immigration officials targeted Asian Indians seeking admission to the United States. Between 1908 and 1920, they denied entry to some 3,453 Asian Indians, most of them on the grounds they would likely become public charges [welfare recipients]. In an article on "The Hindu, the Newest Immigration Problem," *Survey* magazine editorialized in 1910: "The civic and social question concerns the ability of the nation to assimilate this class of Hindus and their probable effect on the communities where they settle. Their habits, their intense caste feeling, their lack of home life—no women being among them—and their effect upon standards of labor and wages, all combine to raise a serious question as to whether the doors should be kept open or closed against this strange, new stream." Seven years later, Congress enacted an immigration restriction law which designated India as one of the Asian countries in the "barred zone" and prohibited the entry of Asian-Indian laborers. . . .

At Work on Railroads and Farms

While Asian-Indian immigrants were interested in political developments in their homeland, most of them were mainly concerned about their condition in America. They had come with high hopes. "The Indian journals have been full of stories of the splendid opportunities to make money by ordinary work," reported the Reverend E.M. Wherry. "Men, receiving from 5 to 8 cents a day in India, were told that by emigrating to America they might become suddenly rich. . . . There are now thousands of these Hindu peasants who have pushed their way into America." They had hoped they would soon make their fortunes by working in the fruit orchards and sawmills at from seventy-five cents to two dollars a day.

Most of the Asian-Indian immigrants had been farmers or farm laborers in the Punjab. Eighty percent came from the *jat*, or farmer caste. Shortly after their arrival, however, many Asian Indians were first employed as railroad workers. Seven hundred were reportedly involved in the construction of the Three-Mile Spring Garden Tunnel of the Western Pacific Railroad. In Tacoma, Washington, Asian Indians were used as replacements for Italian railroad strikers. . . .

Increasingly Asian Indians found themselves driven from employment in the railroad and lumber industries by violent white workers, and they moved south, riding the Southern Pacific Railroad into California, where they found employment in agriculture. "Every train that comes from the North and passes this city," commented the *Red Bluff News* in 1907 in a report on the movement of Asian Indians into the state, "has from one to twenty and often more of this new pest." Many California farmers, however, were eager to hire Asian Indians. The Chinese Exclusion Act had prohibited the entry of Chinese workers, and the Gentlemen's Agreement[1] had cut off the

1. A 1908 agreement between Japan and the United States in which Japan agreed to deny passports to Japanese workers intending to enter the U.S. and recognizing the U.S. right to exclude Japanese holiday passports originally issued for other countries.

supply of Japanese labor, so farmers turned to Asian Indians to reduce the labor shortage. "With the number of Japanese and Chinese laborers diminishing as a result of the restrictions placed upon the immigration of these classes," observed Immigration Commission Superintendent H.A. Millis in 1912, "the East Indians with freer immigration might fall heir to the kinds of work which have been done in part by these other Asiatics; for employers are inclined to follow the line of least resistance in finding a supply of labor, and competition between races engaged in unskilled work apparently depends more upon the rate of wages than upon efficiency." Indeed, farmers paid Asian-Indian workers from twenty-five to fifty cents less per day than Japanese laborers and used them to keep wages down.

In northern California, five hundred Punjabis initially worked in the Newcastle fruit district east of Sacramento in 1908, and three hundred compatriots picked fruit in the nearby Vaca Valley. Asian-Indian farm laborers quickly spread throughout the Sacramento Valley, working on fruit farms and rice farms near Marysville, Tudor, Willows, and Chico. They moved into the San Joaquin Valley, where they worked in the grape and celery fields and where they cleared lands for new fields. Some six hundred of them were employed on the Tulare citrus farms. From the San Joaquin Valley, Asian Indians entered the Imperial Valley, gathering cantaloupes and picking cotton. A grower told an interviewer in 1930: "We are using Hindus for cleaning our ditches. The Japs won't do it and the Chinese have gotten too old. You can't get the younger generations of these peoples into any of this common work. But the Hindus are very efficient at this work." . . .

Travelling in gangs from farm to farm, Punjabi laborers worked from ten to fourteen hours a day, depending on the season and the type of crop. [Stated laborer Dhan Gopal Mukerji], "We got up at half past three," said one of them describing work in the asparagus fields, "and before the first faint daylight was visible we were ready for work." The workers were given miles and miles of rows. Cutting asparagus was monotonous and repetitious. "As soon as I had knelt down with my knife and cut out one head and put it in the box, there would be another one sprouting before me. Then I would have to stoop again, and it was this continuous picking and stooping that made it a terrible form of exercise." All day long it was "walk and bend, bend and walk," from half past four in the morning until seven in the evening. Periodically the boss—"an American foreman"—would come into the asparagus fields and yell, "Hurry up! Hurry up!"

The Race Riot Against the East Indians of Washington

Joan M. Jensen

The East Indian immigrants who came to the West Coast of the United States and Canada in the early 1900s were primarily Sikhs from the Punjab, a region of northern India. These unskilled laborers found work in the lumber mills of northern California, Oregon, Washington State, and British Columbia. They also worked on the railroads in the Pacific Northwest and in California. The Sikh workers were resented by the labor unions in the Pacific Northwest and by whites who wanted to protect jobs from the competition posed by cheap Indian labor. In 1907 the Japanese and Korean Exclusion League of San Francisco renamed itself the Asian Exclusion League (AEL) to include Indians in its plan to oppose Asian immigration. The AEL warned Americans that East Indians were not to be trusted. As historian Joan M. Jensen describes in this selection, that same year the AEL played a leading role in fomenting racial attacks against East Indians living in Bellingham, Washington.

The Bellingham race riot was the result of simmering labor unrest in the Pacific Northwest in the early 1900s as well as racial prejudice against Asians. When the East Indian men showed up for work in the town, they were harassed and physically attacked by white workers. In the ensuing violence a mob of several hundred white workers and townspeople attacked the houses of the East Indian workers, wrecked them, and drove the Indians out of town.

Jensen is professor emerita of history at New Mexico State University. She is the author of Promise to the Land: Essays on Rural Women *and* With These Hands: Women Working on the Land.

Joan M. Jensen, *Passage from India: Asian Indian Immigrants in North America.* New Haven, CT: Yale University Press, 1988, pp. 42–49. Copyright © 2004 by Yale University. All rights reserved. Reproduced by permission.

As Indians moved into Washington state to work in lumber mills and on the railroads, they came into contact with Euro-American workers already locked in combat with employers over issues of wages and working conditions. The employers welcomed the new group of Asians, who could be used to undercut these organizing efforts. The presence of even a small number of Asian workers increased the high level of tension already present in the Pacific Northwest. First at Bellingham, then at Vancouver, and later in a series of smaller towns as far up and down the coast as Juneau, Alaska, and Live Oak, California, groups of Euro-American workers responded to Indians by organizing to drive them away. These expulsions eventually pushed Indians out of many areas and jobs in Washington, Oregon, and much of northern California, forcing their retreat into agricultural regions of central California where other Indians had already settled, Euro-American workers had not yet organized, and growers were expanding their operations.

The expulsions—in fact small riots directed against the presence of Indians in communities in the Northwest—fit well into the typology of riots developed by the sociologist Otto Dalke, who found that there are certain prerequisites for the occurrence of a riot. First, the community usually must be in transition. The subordinate group—in this case Asians—must have a history of being victims of violence, must be regarded as undesirable competitors, and must exhibit some trait or characteristic that can serve as a focal point for negative assessments. Established authorities usually must tacitly support violence or refuse to assume responsibility for riot control. An association devoted to propaganda or advocating violence against the minority group usually must exist, with a press that enforces the association's negative assessments. Finally, the upper and middle classes must either stand by or encourage violence. All these situations were present in 1907, when the major riots and expulsions of Indians took place in the Pacific Northwest.

Bellingham in 1907

The communities in which these riots occurred were in an extreme period of economic and social transition when the first Indians arrived. Bellingham, a frontier town fifty miles south of Vancouver and linked to it by the Great Northern Railway, had a burst of population in the first years of the century similar to that of Vancouver. Salmon, trees, and coal brought men to Bellingham Bay in the late nineteenth century. In 1903, four clapboard villages along the sea joined to form a town, which in the next three years shot up to a population of over thirty thousand. The new town served as a distribution center for Whatcom County and an industrial center of mines, canneries, and mills. A park with a roller coaster and an opera house made the town a social center as well. "Our community is composed of men who accomplish results," boasted Mayor Alfred L. Black. "There is plenty of room for more of that class." The Pacific Northwest brought quick profits for some, disillusionment for others. Railroads and lumbering provided much the same incentive for young men to go west as had the gold rush fifty years earlier. Boom conditions in the summer of 1907 brought hordes of young men, most under age twenty-five, to the mill camps bordering the railroad. Overcrowded, buggy, and unsanitary, the camps bred disillusionment. The men, often migrants, were discontented and frustrated, outcasts of the working class who nevertheless considered themselves protectors of the frontier tradition of white supremacy.

These Euro-American newcomers had the potential for hostility to Asians, and they were entering a West that already had a tradition of violence against Asian immigrants, particularly the Chinese. Hostility toward Chinese had already been growing for more than a decade when, in 1873, Euro-American workers joined race and class antagonisms in a violent outbreak against Chinese workers. Many of the fifty thousand Euro-Americans who had been enticed west by low railway fares and an economic depression on the East Coast became convinced by nativists that Chinese immigrants were unfairly competing for the jobs they themselves sought. Sporadic violence against the Chinese continued for the next twenty years, culminating in the Chinese Exclusion Act of 1882, which began a century-long policy restricting Asian immigration.

Anti-Asian Sentiments

National legislation did not halt the violence, however. In 1885, white workers chased Chinese workers out of thirty-five small California communities, such as Chico and Eureka. White miners massacred Chinese miners in Wyoming, and mobs in Tacoma, Seattle, and Bellingham drove Chinese immigrants out of Washington. Anti-Chinese riots occurred throughout the Puget Sound area in 1886. Chinese were driven from camps and terrorized in Vancouver. By 1907, Chinese were allowed into Bellingham only during fishing season, when their labor was needed in the salmon canneries. Violence against Japanese workers was much less widespread, in part because Japanese officials were more active in defending their nationals, and in part because Japanese immigrants were more militant in defending themselves. When white mill hands at Bellingham attempted to expel Japanese lumbermen, the Japanese armed themselves and threatened retaliation. Rather than risk open warfare, the whites acquiesced, and by 1907, Japanese workers constituted about 5 percent of lumbermen in the Bellingham area.

By 1907, there was also an association dedicated to organizing opposition to Asian immigration. At first called the Japanese and Korean Exclusion League, the organization was soon renamed the Asiatic Exclusion League (AEL) to include Indians among its targets. The stated goals of the league were not to encourage violence but rather to create and focus hostility against Asians in order to influence officials to exclude Asians. However, the actual tactics of the AEL, especially arranging parades to bring together hostile workers, were calculated to motivate people to act on their hostility toward Asians. Many of the leaders of the AEL were also leaders in the organized labor movement and thus had access to networks through which they could spread anti-Asian arguments, goals, and plans. The combination was a volatile one.

Moreover, neither the police nor their middle-class employers in the Northwest were convinced that Asians should remain. While there is no evidence that police joined anti-Asian mobs, they did allow mobs to expel Asians from several areas. Policemen no doubt protected some individual Asians from beatings, but they did not protect them from harassment and expulsion. Added to police inaction was the attitude of the middle class in Northwestern communities. Holding a precarious position at best in a sea of working-class men, the middle class was unsure not only of its own sentiments toward Asians but also of what opposition to Asian exclusion might mean for business and political careers. When owners needed Asian labor badly and Euro-American labor was difficult to find, employers lauded Asian workers. When Euro-American workers organized against owners who employed Asians, the employers were more hesitant. Political leaders valued workers' votes. Social leaders feared workers' potential for violence in western boom towns.

The Turban and What It Represented

Perhaps the most important physical characteristic that helped exclusionists focus hostility on Indians was the turban. Chinese had become "Chinks" in exclusionist rhetoric; Japanese had become "Japs." Indians became "rag-heads." Because most Indians were Caucasians, their features were less likely to distinguish them even with brown skins. Some Indians, in fact, found that they could discard their turbans and pass as southern Italians or Portuguese. But for Sikhs and other men trying to maintain their religious and cultural identity, the turban was an essential symbol. They would not abandon it. Much of the animosity thus came to be focused on the turban and on a cluster of complaints about cultural patterns that exclusionists associated with the turban. Much of the hostility, however, was an outgrowth of deep-seated and long-standing animosities already in place against Chinese and Japanese. The Indian was labeled an "Asiatic," one of the hordes of potential competitors in a job market already depressed, volatile, and difficult to organize.

The attitudes of white workers were bitter and would remain so into the 1920s. "One of these days, by God," swore one disgruntled lumber piler interviewed later, "the whites are going to chase all of them out of camp and they won't come back either. We'll drive them all down the line with a two-by-four. If the whites only knew enough to stick together and organize we wouldn't need to work with those damned Orientals."

Union representatives championed workers' opposition to the employment of Indians, arguing that the shortage of American labor was only temporary. If Indians established themselves in the mills, the union men argued, they would provide strong competition for white workers. Late in August 1907, mill workers warned all owners that they must not employ Indians after Labor Day, September 2. On Labor Day, a thousand unionists paraded down the main streets of Bellingham to show their solidarity. It is difficult to see how the subsequent riots in Bellingham could have been avoided, given all the elements that presaged violent conflict.

The Riot Begins

The day before the Bellingham parade, Indians congregated in one of the main streets. Workers later claimed that women were crowded off the streets. After the parade several Indians were beaten, ostensibly in defense of "white womanhood." Nevertheless, on Tuesday morning the Indians showed up for work as usual. All day, white mill workers continued to complain. That night five instances of violence against Indians were reported to the police. Windows in two Indians' houses were smashed. The police chief ignored the evidence of growing violence; he assigned no extra deputies and made no special report to the mayor. The Bellingham police force was understaffed, with only nine men for a population of more than thirty thousand.

On Wednesday, mill hands circulated an informal notice: meet to "drive out the Hindus." That evening, two Indians walking along C Street were attacked, knocked down, and beaten. One attempted to escape onto a streetcar but was dragged off. Both men managed to flee into the water of nearby tidal flats, where two young men pelted them with stones. Meanwhile, workmen collected to encourage the harassment. Speakers fanned the indignation of the crowd with impromptu speeches urging them to "help drive out the cheap labor." By the time the police chief and a patrolman arrived, the mob had grown to several hundred workers and townspeople. The police arrested and handcuffed the two youths who were stoning the Indians. The mob surrounded the police and demanded that the boys be released. Four more policemen arrived. Two-thirds of the entire force was now on the scene. Later the chief said he feared that bloodshed would have followed arrests. He released the two youths. Stepping back, he simply cautioned the rioters against violence.

Assured of the acquiesence of the police, the mob—now five hundred strong—swept down to the waterfront barracks where many of the Indians lived. Battering down the doors, the mob threw belongings into the street, pocketed money and jewelry, and dragged Indians from their beds. The Indians fled, some injuring themselves by jumping from buildings in an attempt to escape. Those who did not move fast enough were beaten. One landlord turned out four Indians to protect his boarding house from damage. Rioters attacked a tenement on Forest Street, roused the occupants, and forced them into the street. Fifty men stormed the surrounding mills, pulled Indians from their bunks, and began to burn bunkhouses. To avoid further physical violence, the police chief turned over the red-roofed, turreted city hall to the rioters to hold Indians. By morning over two hundred Indians were jammed into the city hall. At dawn, the tired revelers dispersed. From that time on, as one reporter wryly commented, "the police had the situation well in hand." Police held the Indians in custody as the city council arrived to hold a special session. Three Sikhs—Nand Singh, Attar Singh, and Sergent Singh—were allowed to appear before the council in the morning.

Many Indians Leave

Mayor Black, conspicuously absent the evening before, now assured the three tall bearded men who solemnly stated their grievances that they would be protected. Black lectured his council. "They have the legal right to be in this city so long as they do not infringe upon the laws thereof. I do not think that there is any charge that these men have broken any law of our state or city, and therefore they have a legal right to remain in this city and perform any occupation that they see fit. They have a right to the protection of the laws of this state and city, so long as they do not break those laws." Then turning to the Sikhs, he assured them: "The entire force of this city and of the state, if necessary, will be called on to protect you in doing anything that you may see fit in this city, so long as you abide by the laws of the state and of the city." The mayor asked Thomas to swear in fifty deputies to prevent further rioting, and the police chief promised to arrest some of the rioters that he could identify himself. The council seemed most concerned about the mill owners, but promised to investigate the cause of the riots and to report at a meeting the following Monday evening.

The mill owners all vowed to protect their property and to defend their employees from the mill hands. A few owners said that they did not want the Indians in town, openly calling them undesirable citizens and laborers. One owner told the council that the problem would be eliminated if "white" men could be secured for the low-paying jobs instead of Indians. Larson's Mill, one of the largest in the country, announced that it would shut down anyway because the eastern market was closing up as a result of a financial panic. Another large employer of Indians outside of town discharged them all because, he said, he feared his mill would be burned. Even though some mill owners offered them wages equal to the whites', the Indians were ready to leave town. Many had already gathered together what they could find of their meager possessions—little brass lamps, brass kettles, coffee pots, clothes, blankets—and started up the railroad tracks that led back to British Columbia. Others waited until police escorted them to collect back pay from the mills and to withdraw savings from the bank before trudging down to the station to wait for the next northbound train. Crowds of townspeople jeered them off on the Great Northern.

Bellingham Leaders Approve of the Riot

Despite promises of protection by the mayor, there was a growing undercurrent of approval in the white community for the sentiment behind the actions of the mob, if not for the riot itself. The Bellingham *Herald* carried an editorial, titled "A Public Disgrace," condemning the riot but supporting the ideology of white supremacy. "It is simply a question of whether the people of this city are to deal with all questions that arise in a dignified manner, in keeping with the restriction placed upon them by law, or whether they shall, whenever the whim strikes them, convert this into a lawless frontier settlement," wrote the editor. One reporter even condemned the police force. "The turning over of the jail to the men is regarded as the strangest piece of work ever performed in any city in the country." Police could simply have closed the doors and had most of the mob in jail, he observed. These journalists felt that although the method had been wrong, the sentiment had been right. It was not bitter racial hatred that motivated the crowd but a "half-humorous spirit," wrote the editor. "The Hindu is not a good citizen," he concluded. "It would require centuries to assimilate him, and this country need not take the trouble. Our racial burdens are already heavy enough to bear. . . . Our cloak of brotherly love is not large enough to include him as a member of the body politic." . . .

Sentiment began to shift from support for the rights of the Indians to support for exclusion. Newspapers reported rumors that Indians had been bold and insolent, had insulted women in streetcars and pushed them into gutters. Indar Singh, spokesman for the Bellingham Indian community, announced on Friday that all his countrymen would be gone before Saturday morning. Once the Indians had decided to leave, the police chief proclaimed the troubles over. Five alleged rioters were arrested on Friday, including one hack driver and one shingle-weaver, but there were no prosecutions. The riot had been successful, even if, as some still thought, regrettable.

The Gadar Movement Calls for Indians to Fight the British

Ved Prakash Vatuk

The Gadar movement was founded by Punjabi Indians in San Francisco in 1913. Gadar (also spelled Ghadar or Ghadr is an Urdu word meaning "revolution" or "uprising." The leaders of the Gadar movement wanted Indian workers, farmers, and students in the United States and Canada to return to India and fight for independence from its British rulers. The Gadarites opposed British rule for many political, economic, and cultural reasons, but they were especially angered by the failure of British consular officials in the United States to speak out on the behalf of Indians attacked by American mobs. The Gadar members also believed that the British would persuade America's political leaders to oppose further Indian immigration.

As poet, essayist, and folklorist Ved Prakash Vatuk describes in this selection, when the United States entered World War I in 1917, its ally Great Britain pressured the United States to keep a close watch on its Indian immigrants. The United States also decided to prosecute Gadar leaders who were fomenting revolt against Britain's rule in India and helping Britain's wartime enemy, Germany. As thousands of East Indians returned to India to carry out the revolution against British rule, many were jailed and executed, Vatuk writes. Nonetheless, many East Indians stayed loyal to the cause of revolution and continued to work toward its goals.

Vatuk has taught at the University of California at Berkeley and at the University of Chicago. He is also a contributing author to the Encyclopedia of Hinduism.

Ved Prakash Vatuk, foreword to F.C. Isemonger and J. Slattery, *An Account of the Ghadr Conspiracy (1913–1915)*. Punjab, Lahore: Government Printing, 1919; repr., Folklore Institute of Berkeley, 1998, pp. v–xii. www.sikhpioneers.org//forward.html.

India's economy was thoroughly shattered by the end of the nineteenth century. Even the villages in Punjab did not remain untouched by this ruin. Peasantry was becoming poorer and debt-ridden day by day due to the zamindari system.[1] So much so that there were only two ways remaining by which young men of the state could escape the horror of poverty—enlisting in the armed forces or emigrating to other countries. Some Indian soldiers, who had fought bravely on the side of the British in various battles, were invited to England to take part in the fiftieth anniversary celebration of the rule of Queen Victoria [in 1887]. They were also given the opportunity to visit Canada before returning to India. In Canada, they saw the abundance of land. Some of the Punjabis had also read or heard what the scholars of Vedant Movements [religious movements through which Hinduism was introduced to Westerners] like Swami Ram Tirth have written about America. Hundreds of young men dreamt to leave their homes and try their luck in the far away unknown land. From their village they went on foot or by carts to the nearest railway station, took the train to Calcutta where they boarded a ship carrying them to Hong Kong or some other port in South East Asia. From there they took another ship to journey across the Atlantic Ocean landing in Vancouver, Canada or in San Francisco, USA. Many sold their land to pay for the fare. It took them a long time to reach their destination. For example, a prominent freedom fighter of the Gadar Party, Harnam Singh Tundilat, left his home on May 12, 1906 and reached Canada on July 12, 1906. With him there were only 22 Punjabi travelers in the ship. That was the largest number of Indians by that time who traveled by any ship to America. In years to follow the number went up. In some ships there were seven to eight hundred Indians traveling to North America. Gradually the

1. A system of landownership and tax collection in India during the Mughal period (1526–1857). During British rule, the Zamindars, or landlords, collected taxes on lands rented out to peasants. The taxes were turned over to the British, and the Zamindar kept a portion for himself.

number of Indians who migrated to Canada or the USA reached thirteen thousand by 1913. Ninety per cent of them were Sikh from Punjab. They settled down on the West Coast.

Unwelcome Newcomers

A few travelers among them could read or write Urdu or Punjabi written in Gurumukhi [the Punjabi script]. But their aim was simply to earn and save enough money to buy some land. They could earn two to three dollars a day. One dollar was equal to three rupees and one and a half annas in those days. In India an elementary school teacher would earn that much in a month what they earned in a day in the USA. Even though these new immigrants proved to be very hard working dedicated workers in the fields and factories, they were not much welcomed by their new nations. Both in Canada and in the USA people got alarmed by this new 'Hindu invasion.' Canada enacted many new laws restricting immigration from Asia. One of them made it mandatory for anyone coming to Canada that he/she should board the ship sailing directly from their own country. Even when a ship, *Komagata Maru*, was charted to sail from India to take its human cargo directly to Vancouver, it was forced to turn back without any of its passengers landing. The ship remained in the harbor for many weeks.

America and Canada were in the grips of racism and segregation in those days. There were separate places for black and white people to live, to go to bathrooms, to eat and to go to school. At every step Indians were insulted. They were called names. Looked down upon. Several times they were chased away from towns and factories. Riots were organized against them. When Japanese workers met such fate the Government of Japan made strong protests to the American Government. But the British Government in India put pressure on America to keep a tight watch on Indians. They should not be infected with the virus of any thoughts of freedom. If possible, they should be kicked out of North America. British

Government sent its own spies to help Canadian and American Governments. Indians soon realized that the main cause of the inhuman treatment they received at the hands of Americans and Canadians was the fact that they came from a subjugated nation. They felt that they would be treated in this way as long as India remained a 'slave' country. A feeling of patriotism and nationalism was born in their heart. They expressed their resentment against the British rule by burning all certificates of appreciation and medals given to them for the bravery in battles in a meeting held in Vancouver in 1909. On the other hand Indian students who were attending American universities at that time also tried to foster feelings of patriotism and nationalism among them. In 1908 Taraknath Das started publishing a paper, *Free Hindustan*. Another Punjabi paper, *Swadesh Sewak*, was started by Gurudutt Kumar. In Europe . . . Indians were working for the cause of India's freedom. Shymji Krishna Varma, who was the founder of Indian Home Rule Society and India House in London was publishing *Indian Sociologist*. Madam Cama was leading a movement for India's freedom in Paris. In Berlin there was a committee active in the same direction. India House organized a meeting to celebrate the 50th anniversary of the 1857 Gadar (the First Indian War for Independence) on May 10, 1908. In this meeting Vir Vinayak Domodar Savarkar declared, "The battle that we started on May 10, 1857 will not end until a day comes when we will be the master of our fate and our motherland becomes free." Lala Har Dayal was also present in that meeting. He had joined the freedom movement after renouncing a fellowship to study at Oxford University. Three years later Lala Har Dayal came to the USA to join Stanford University where he taught Indian philosophy. His fame had reached far and wide among academic circles. Har Dayal inspired many students who were studying at the University of California at Berkeley at the time. Prominent among them were Katar Singh Sarabha, Vishnu Govind Pingle and D. Chenchiah. Katar Singh

Sarabha was a remarkable young man. He was at ease in the company of peasants as well as among intellectuals. He worked hard in the fields and at his studies. He ran the printing press, wrote articles and poems, learnt how to fly a plane and studied engineering. He was a link between the workers and intellectuals, between Har Dayal and other future leaders of Gadar Party. It was with his great efforts that a meeting of Indians from all walks of life took place in Astoria, Oregon in April 1913. The meeting was addressed by Har Dayal and Bhai Parmanand. It was in this meeting that an association—Hindi Association of the Pacific Coast—was formed. Sohan Singh Bhakna was elected its first president, Har Dayal was elected secretary and the position of treasurer was given to Pandit Kashi Ram.

From Hindi Association to Gadar

The aim of this association was to foster a feeling of nationalism among Indians which would prepare them for an armed revolution to make India free. San Francisco was chosen to be the city of its headquarters. The headquarters was named Yugantar Ashram after a revolutionary Bengali paper, *Yugantar*. To keep alive the memory of [the] 1857 revolution it was decided to launch a weekly in several Indian languages. The weekly was named *Gadar*. The first issue of the *Gadar* was published in Urdu on November 1, 1913 from 5 Wood Street, San Francisco. Under the heading 'Our Name, Our Work', it declared: "A new calendar is launched in the history of India today on November 1, 1913, alien land in our native language. It is an auspicious day that a paper in Urdu and Gurumukhi is launched to root out the British evil (from our country)".

Further it wrote: "What is our name? 'Gadar'. What is our work? 'Gadar'. "Our name and our work is the same. No need to fuss about it. . . . Where will this Gadar take place? In India. When? Very soon. Why will it take place? Because the people are fed up with British Rule's tyranny and are ready to die fighting for their freedom." Under the "Wanted Ads" it published: "Wanted: brave young men/revolutionaries, job: to launch gadar, pay: martyrdom, reward: India's freedom".

Gadar was edited, printed and published from the Yugantar Ashram. All the people who were connected with it lived in the Ashram. So did the persons who carried [on] the day-to-day work for the association. It was a communal living—people lived there in a democratic way in a life style based on equality and devoid of any casteism, racism, religious bigotry and sectarianism of any kind. All those who lived there were just Indian. They cooked, ate and lived together like a family. They were the followers of one path. Maulana Barkatullah, Lala Har Dayal, Raghubar Dayal Gupta and the rest all got the same food, clothing and two dollars a month pocket money. They greeted each other by saying *Bande Mataram* [the title of a patriotic song]. For this privilege many people left their well-paying jobs, their farms, their property. They gave all they had to the association in order to come to live and to work in the Ashram. All waited for the time to come when they will replace their pens with guns and fight in the battlefield.

The Growth of the Gadar Movement

Gadar exposed the British Rule. *Gadar* gave the call for a revolution. It was a people's paper in every sense of the word. It carried articles of intellectuals like Har Dayal, serialized the history of [the] 1857 Gadar by Savarkar, and published the folk poetry written in direct and revolutionary style. Its publication was like a bomb-shell. Copies were sent free to all countries wherever Indians lived—in all continents. It became so popular and its demand so great that the association itself came to be known as Gadar Party and its headquarters became famous as Gadar Ashram. Money poured. Workers gave almost half of their salaries. *Gadar* was published for four years regularly. Then it became irregular. In 1925 a special issue was published. The last issue available today in Punjabi was published in 1929. Poems published in the *Gadar* became so popular that they were printed and distributed again and again in book form as *Gadar-Di-Gunj*. They were memorized and recited in all kinds of rallies and conventions. Gadar Party also published many books exposing the evils of the British Rule.

This all happened so fast that the British Government got very alarmed. They began to put pressure on America to arrest and jail Har Dayal and declare him to be an anarchist and a terrorist. Har Dayal was arrested and released on bail on March 24, 1914. [He] left America for Switzerland. If the British Government had thought that by removing Har Dayal from the scene it would be able to kill the Gadar Movement, it couldn't be more mistaken. As a matter of fact, it made the people more determined, angrier than ever. They were more committed to the cause.

World War I

When the World War I broke out, the gadarites felt that it was the golden opportunity to throw the British out of India. They began to establish contacts with various nations. They called upon Indians to get ready to go to India and launch the revolution. They wanted to go and infiltrate the army in India and tell Indian soldiers that instead of fighting to save [the] British empire they should wage battle against the British to free India. They wanted to eliminate British officers in India, free political prisoners, rob government treasuries, disrupt means of communications and transportation, train young people for the revolution and organize the people—the peasants and workers. Big rallies were held in many American cities. Members of the Gadar Party began to return home in large numbers by whatever ship they could get. Arms were collected and shipped. It was all done openly. Spies of the British Government were also busy. By the time all was said and done, almost six thousand Indians left for India. The British Government of India was truly alarmed. Their faith in Punjabi soldiers was shaken. Even before the gadarites reached India, eight thousand Punjabi soldiers were given leave, five thousand were expelled from the army, four hundred were jailed and thousands were put under house arrest in their own villages. The British Government was ready to face the gadarites when they reached India. Many of them were arrested as soon as they set their foot on Indian soil. Trains were ready to take them directly to Punjab and to prisons. Many of them were shot dead on the spot. It will never be known how many of them lost their lives at the hands of the British. Thousands of them were put under house arrest after they were taken to their villages.

The atmosphere in India was also not in their favor. People were not ready to take advantage of the situation and throw the British out. Nor were their leaders. Leaders of the Congress Party [the political party that worked for India's independence] such as Moti Lal Nehru, and Mahatma Gandhi were actively helping the British in recruiting soldiers. The native kings and princes, in whom gadarites put so much faith, turned out to be stooges of the British and the religious leaders issued *fatwas* [an Islamic decree] against them, excommunicated and expelled them from their faith, branded them traitors. Gurudwaras [Sikh places of worship] and temples, churches and mosques were all filled with those who prayed for the victory of the British. In spite of all odds, some brave people escaped the British net and reached their destination. They tried to organize the workers, made contracts with soldiers in various barracks. They also made alliances with revolutionaries in other states such as Ras Behari Bose and Shachindra Sanyal. They came to the conclusion that in many cantonments [military bases] soldiers were very dissatisfied and could revolt. Kartar Singh Sarabha and Vishnu Govind Pingle were very active in that mission. After establishing contacts with many soldiers, a date was fixed to launch a revolt. But they were betrayed by some spies among them. And they along with many soldiers were arrested. Even so, there were several regiments outside India who did revolt.

On Trial

Gadarites, who were arrested and jailed at various places, were tried in several trials. Among them, the most famous are trials held at Lahore. Many of them were hanged, and scores of them were given *kala pani* [solitary confinement]. Among those who were hanged were 19-year-old Kartar Singh Sarabha and 23-year-old Visnu Govind Pingle. Even when they were being led to the hanging place, they sang patriotic songs. Those who were sent to rot in Andaman Nicobar's cellular jail for life, waged wars against the most inhuman conditions in that prison. Many of them went again and again on hunger strikes lasting several weeks, suffered tortures, beatings, placements in cages shackled and handcuffed. . . . Many of them died there during those struggles for prison-reforms. When some of them were released from these hells, they came out more determined than ever. All their life they remained truthful to the spirit of the revolution and worked hard for it.

East Indians Are Declared Ineligible for U.S. Citizenship

George Sutherland

In the early 1900s various factions on the West Coast of the United States opposed East Indian immigration. One of these groups was the Asian Exclusion League (AEL) of San Francisco, which sought to keep Asian immigrants, including East Indians, Chinese, Japanese, and Koreans out of the United States. Discrimination against Asians led to the Immigration Act of 1917, which banned immigration to the United States from Asian countries. The 1917 law also raised a legal debate over whether East Indians were to be considered Asian or white. Racially, East Indians are Caucasian like Europeans, though they have dark skin. In the view of the U.S. government, Caucasian *meant "white," and any person who was white was allowed to be naturalized. People thus began to debate whether a person belonging to a group excluded by the Immigration Act should be allowed to become a citizen.*

The following selection is excerpted from a landmark Supreme Court ruling in a case involving an East Indian immigrant who applied for citizenship. Born in India's Punjab region in 1892, Bhagat Singh Thind came to the United States in 1913, attended the University of California, and served in the U.S. Army during World War I. In 1920 when he applied for citizenship while a resident of Oregon, his application was approved by the district court. However, in 1923 the U.S. Supreme Court ordered the revocation of Thind's citizenship certificate. In his majority opinion statement, Justice George Sutherland writes that while Indians are Caucasian in the anthropological sense, they are not white in the "common man's understanding" of the word and therefore were never intended to be naturalized. Sutherland

George Sutherland, Supreme Court decision in *U.S. v. Bhagat Singh Thind*, 261–U.S. 204, 1923.

also notes that since Congress had already passed the 1917 law rejecting Asian immigration, it was not likely that Congress would then accept East Indians as citizens.

Thind remained in the United States despite the decision against him and applied for his citizenship through the state of New York a few years after the Supreme Court's ruling. He continued his studies, earned a doctorate, and lectured and wrote widely on the subject of metaphysics. In 1946 the Thind *decision was reversed and the Asian American Citizenship Act was signed into law. The act allowed Asians to become naturalized citizens and set quotas for Indian immigration at one hundred per year.*

Mr. Justice SUTHERLAND delivered the opinion of the Court.

This cause is here upon a certificate from the Circuit Court of Appeals requesting the instruction of this Court in respect of the following questions:

1. Is a high-caste Hindu, of full Indian blood, born at Amritsar, Punjab, India, a white person within the meaning of section 2169, Revised Statutes?

2. Does the Act of February 5, 1917 (39 Stat. 875, 3), disqualify from naturalization as citizens those Hindus now barred by that act, who had lawfully entered the United States prior to the passage of said act? . . .

On Citizenship for Whites

Section 2169, Revised Statutes, provides that the provisions of the Naturalization Act[1] 'shall apply to aliens being free white persons and to aliens of African nativity and to persons of African descent.'

If the applicant is a white person, within the meaning of this section, he is entitled to naturalization; otherwise not. In

1. Sutherland is referring to the Naturalization Act of 1795, which extended naturalization to free, white persons, and to the 1870 Page Act, which allowed for the naturalization of aliens of African birth and to persons of African descent.

Ozawa v. United States, decided November 13, 1922, we had occasion to consider the application of these words to the case of a cultivated Japanese and were constrained to hold that he was not within their meaning. As there pointed out, the provision is not that any particular class of persons shall be excluded, but it is, in effect, that only white persons shall be included within the privilege of the statute. The intention was to confer the privilege of citizenship upon that class of persons whom the fathers knew as white, and to deny it to all who could not be so classified. It is not enough to say that the framers did not have in mind the brown or yellow races of Asia. It is necessary to go farther and be able to say that had these particular ... races been suggested, the language of the act would have been so varied as to include them within its privileges—citing *Dartmouth College v. Woodward.* Following a long line of decisions of the lower Federal courts, we held that the words imported a racial and not an individual test and were meant to indicate only persons of what is popularly known as the Caucasian race. But, as there pointed out, the conclusion that the phrase 'white persons' and the word 'Caucasian' are synonymous does not end the matter. It enabled us to dispose of the problem as it was there presented, since the applicant for citizenship clearly fell outside the zone of debatable ground on the negative side; but the decision still left the question to be dealt with, in doubtful and different cases, by the 'process of judicial inclusion and exclusion.' Mere ability on the part of an applicant for naturalization to establish a line of descent from a Caucasian ancestor will not ipso facto and necessarily conclude the inquiry. 'Caucasian' is a conventional word of much flexibility, as a study of the literature dealing with racial questions will disclose, and while it and the words 'white persons' are treated as synonymous for the purposes of that case, they are not of identical meaning— *idem per idem.*

Associate Justice George Sutherland delivered the landmark decision in U.S. v. Bhagat Singh Thind, *which denied citizenship to East Indians.* Photograph by Harris and Ewing. Collection of the Supreme Court of the United States.

The Popular Meaning of 'Caucasian'

In the endeavor to ascertain the meaning of the statute we must not fail to keep in mind that it does not employ the word 'Caucasian,' but the words 'white persons,' and these are words of common speech and not of scientific origin. The word 'Caucasian,' not only was not employed in the law but was probably wholly unfamiliar to the original framers of the statute in 1790. When we employ it, we do so as an aid to the ascertainment of the legislative intent and not as an invariable substitute for the statutory words. Indeed, as used in the science of ethnology, the connotation of the word is by no means clear, and the use of it in its scientific sense as an equivalent for the words of the statute, other considerations aside, would simply mean the substitution of one perplexity for another. But in this country, during the last half century especially, the word by common usage has acquired a popular meaning, not clearly defined, to be sure, but sufficiently so to enable us to say that its popular as distinguished from its scientific application is of appreciably narrower scope. It is in the popular sense of the word, therefore, that we employ it as an aid to the construction of the statute, for it would be obviously illogical to convert words of common speech used in a statute into words of scientific terminology when neither the latter nor the science for whose purposes they were coined was within the contemplation of the framers of the statute or of the people for whom it was framed. The words of the statute are to be interpreted in accordance with the understanding of the common man from whose vocabulary they were taken.

Unmistakable and Profound Differences

They imply, as we have said, a racial test; but the term 'race' is one which, for the practical purposes of the statute, must be applied to a group of living persons now possessing in common the requisite characteristics, not to groups of persons who are supposed to be or really are descended from some remote, common ancestor, but who, whether they both resemble him to a greater or less extent, have, at any rate, ceased altogether to resemble one another. It may be true that the blond Scandinavian and the brown Hindu have a common ancestor in the dim reaches of antiquity, but the average man knows perfectly well that there are unmistakable and profound differences between them to-day; . . .

The eligibility of this applicant [Bhagat Singh Thind] for citizenship is based on the sole fact that he is of high-caste Hindu stock, born in Punjab, one of the extreme northwestern districts of India, and classified by certain scientific authorities as of the Caucasian or Aryan race. The Aryan theory as a racial basis seems to be discredited by most, if not all, modern writers on the subject of ethnology. . . .

The term 'Aryan' has to do with linguistic, and not at all with physical characteristics, and it would seem reasonably clear that mere resemblance in language, indicating a common linguistic root buried in remotely ancient soil, is altogether inadequate to prove common racial origin. There is, and can be, no assurance that the so-called Aryan language was not spoken by a variety of races living in proximity to one another. Our own history has witnessed the adoption of the English tongue by millons of Negroes, whose descendants can never be classified racially with the descendants of white persons, notwithstanding both may speak a common root language. . . .

'Hindus Are Distinct'

What we now hold is that the words 'free white person' are words of common speech, to be interpreted in accordance with the understanding of the common man, synonymous with the word 'Caucasian' only as that word is popularly understood. As so understood and used, whatever may be the speculations of the ethnologist, it does not include the body of people to whom the appellee belongs. It is a matter of familiar observation and knowledge that the physical group characteristics of the Hindus render them readily distinguishable from the various groups of persons in this country commonly recognized as white. The children of English, French, German, Italian, Scandinavian, and other European parentage, quickly merge into the mass of our population and lose the distinctive hallmarks of their European origin. On the other hand, it cannot be doubted that the children born in this country of Hindu parents would retain indefinitely the clear evidence of their ancestry. It is very far from our thought to suggest the slightest question of racial superiority or inferiority. What we suggest is merely racial difference, and it is of such character and extent that the great body of our people instinctively recognize it and reject the thought of assimilation.

It is not without significance in this connection that Congress, by the [Immigration] Act of February 5, 1917, 39 Stat. 874, c. 29, 3, has now excluded from admission into this country all natives of Asia within designated limits of latitude and longitude, including the whole of India. This not only constitutes conclusive evidence of the congressional attitude of opposition to Asiatic immigration generally, but is persuasive of a similar attitude toward Asiatic naturalization as well, since it is not likely that Congress would be willing to accept as citizens a class of persons whom it rejects as immigrants.

COMING TO
AMERICA

CHAPTER 2

The Second Wave of East Indian Immigrants

Liberalization of U.S. Policies on East Indian Immigration and Naturalization

Gary R. Hess

Prior to World War II, East Indian immigrants in the United States were subject to a variety of laws that kept their numbers low and their status restricted. The most serious restriction was the denial of citizenship requests of East Indians beginning in 1932. Laws in California that prohibited the leasing or sale of land to aliens who were ineligible for citizenship affected most East Indian farmers in California's agricultural regions. Indians in the United States responded to these restrictions by either moving back to India or migrating elsewhere. According to some statistics, the East Indian population in California alone dropped from about 10,000 in 1914 to 3,130 in 1930. In 1940 the East Indian population stood at 2,405 nationwide. As author Gary R. Hess asserts in this selection, the East Indian community in the United States would almost certainly have continued to decrease to the point of disappearance if the events of World War II had not intervened. Hess describes the impact of the war and the changes it brought about in the legal status of East Indians. The U.S. government's policy toward East Indians began to change when it looked to India as a potential ally against Japan's expansionism in Asia. Changes in the laws affecting Chinese immigrants also impacted Indian immigrants. China was defending itself against Japanese aggression and was an ally of the United States in the war. As a result, American exclusionary laws against the Chinese were lifted in 1943, and naturalization was opened to Chinese immigrants. As Hess explains, many in government believed that the same rights of naturalization that were ex-

Gary R. Hess, "The Asian Indian Immigrants in the United States, 1900–1965," in *From India to America: A Brief History of Immigration; Problems of Discrimination; Admission and Assimilation.* La Jolla, Calif.: Population Review Publications, 1982, pp. 32–33.

tended to the Chinese should also be extended to East Indians. In 1944 congressional representative Clare Booth Luce and Emanuel Celler introduced bills that would provide naturalization for East Indians and set quotas for East Indian immigrants. After political wrangling threatened to scuttle the bill, President Harry S. Truman took up its cause, Hess writes. In 1946 Truman signed the bill into law. East Indians living in America were now free to apply for naturalization, and a quota for the immigration of East Indians was established.

Hess is a professor of history at Bowling Green University in Ohio.

World War II proved to be the turning point in American naturalization and immigration policies with respect to India. By bringing India into greater prominence, the war produced a movement to end the restrictive measures which had ended East Indian immigration and denied citizenship. After [the Japanese attack on] Pearl Harbor [in December 1941], India took on new significance to Americans as they sought Indian cooperation in the operations against Japan. Liberal spokesmen and some officials in the State Department and White House looked upon India as the crucial test of the vaguely phrased pledge of self-determination in the Atlantic Charter [a 1941 declaration by Great Britain and the United States]. Political developments in India especially during the critical spring and summer of 1942, were followed closely by the American press, public, and government.

A Policy for India

It was such recognition of nationalism in China and that country's military effort which led to the repeal of the Chinese exclusion laws in 1943. China was granted an immigration quota and its nationals were given naturalization privileges. A number of journalists and Congressmen, who earlier had not been concerned with Indian immigration, soon presented the same arguments in favor of an identical policy for India, since it seemed obvious that independence was only a matter of time and India was making a substantial contribution to the war effort. The movement, however, still faced opposition from those who believed any break in the immigration policy set twenty years earlier was a dangerous precedent.

In Congress, Representatives Emanuel Celler and Clare Booth Luce introduced bills in March, 1944 providing for East Indian naturalization privileges and a quota for Indian immigrants. An alternative measure had been presented three months earlier by Senator William Langer; it provided only for the granting of citizenship to all East Indians who had entered the United States prior to 1924. Although strongly backed by a number of newspapers and a wide range of prominent persons, including [Socialist Labor Party leader] Louis Fisher, [author] Pearl Buck, [theologian] Reinhold Niebuhr, [scientist] Albert Einstein, and [founder of the American Civil Liberties Union] Roger Baldwin, these bills all languished in committee and died with the ending of the Seventy-Eighth Congress.

When the Seventy-Ninth Congress convened in January 1945, these measures were revived and the White House gave support to the broader Celler-Luce approach rather than the more restrictive Langer bill. In the early months of 1945, it appeared certain that the immigration-naturalization bill would pass; on the surface, opposition was minimal. With the backing of the White House and State Department and influential religious and labor groups and with the Chinese example still fresh in mind, it was anticipated that the Celler bill would be reported favorably by the House Immigration Committee. The only outspoken committee critic of the bill, Robert Ramspeck of Georgia, however, quietly rounded up backing for his position among Southern Democrats and Republicans from the Midwest. The coalition organized by Ramspeck succeeded in tabling the bill.

The Role of President Truman

A few weeks later, Harry S. Truman, shortly after succeeding in becoming President, provided leadership in salvaging the Luce-Celler bill. Truman informed Samuel Dickstein, chairman of the House Immigration Committee, of his administration's support and at Celler's urging, the President met with Ramspeck and converted the Congressman from open opposition to acquiesence. This time the Immigration Committee endorsed the bill, and when it was considered by the full House on October 10, supporters dominated the debate and defeated an attempt to send it back to committee. The House approved the bill by a margin of nearly three to one.

Meanwhile in the Senate, the quota and naturalization bills remained in the Immigration Committee. A subcommittee held hearings on Langer's bill in April, but had not reported favorably. Senator Richard B. Russell of Georgia, chairman of the Immigration Committee, was the principal opponent, resisting even Truman's effort to change his position.

Finally in April, 1946, a subcommittee chaired by the freshman Arkansas Senator J. William Fulbright, held hearings on the Celler bill and recommended it to the entire Immigration Committee. Russell, under pressure from Truman and colleagues on the committee, finally permitted the bill to be reported but clearly without his support. When the bill was presented to the Senate, Russell was not present and no opposition was heard. Evident in the comments from the floor in both houses, particularly the Senate, was a willingness to abandon Indian exclusion for a modest quota which would assist the United States interests in Asia. The bill was approved unanimously by the Senate on June 14, 1946. Three weeks later, Truman signed the Indian quota-immigration bill.

After being excluded since 1917, natives of India had been given an annual quota of one hundred. After being denied citizenship since 1923, Indians were now eligible for United States naturalization.

The liberalization of immigration and naturalization policy facilitated an increase in the East Indian community and added immeasurably to its survival and character. Between 1947 and 1965, nearly 6,000 immigrants were admitted to the United States under the quota for India; approximately the same number were also admitted as non-quota immigrants, i.e. husbands, wives and children of American citizens. Between 1948 and 1965, a total of 1,772 persons of former Indian allegiance acquired United States citizenship.

The First East Indian Immigrant to Serve in Congress

Dalip Singh Saund

The passage of the Luce-Celler Act in 1946 allowed East Indian immigrants to become naturalized citizens. Some East Indians already established in the United States were then able to pursue political careers and hold elected office. One, Dalip Singh Saund, became the first East Indian to be elected to the U.S. Congress.

Saund was born in 1899 in the Punjab in India and came to the United States in 1920 to study food preservation at the University of California at Berkeley. After graduation Saund decided to stay in the United States. Settling in the Imperial Valley, Saund became a lettuce farmer. During this time he became active in the Indian American community and spoke out on behalf of Indian independence and citizenship for East Indians in America. Saund first ran for political office in 1949, winning a seat on the local Democratic Central Committee. Then in 1951 he ran for a judgeship and won. Saund ran for Congress in 1956 as a representative from California's 29th district, which included Riverside and Imperial counties. He won that election and served in Congress until 1962. Saund died in 1973.

The following article is taken from Congressman from India, *Saund's autobiography, in which he describes the events surrounding his run for Congress in 1956 and some of the obstacles he had to overcome. He notes how his fellow East Indians doubted his chances of winning and the advantages he gained by having the attention of the media. When his opponent attacked him in the local press, Saund gained valuable publicity and was thrust into the national spotlight when* Time *magazine ran an article about the campaign.*

In mid-November, 1955, one hundred friends from Riverside and Imperial County gathered at Indio, California, and endorsed me as Democratic candidate for Congress in the forthcoming 1956 election. I accepted the endorsement, and from that day on I was an avowed candidate and there was no turning back. While the meeting itself was a source of gratitude and satisfaction to me I realized that these friends of mine had come only to pay a personal tribute. While they were willing to give me all the support they possibly could, I knew they felt deep in their hearts that there really wasn't much chance of my winning the election and going to Congress.

The first big break in my candidacy came a month later. Mr. Phillips, the incumbent congressman, a veteran of forty years of public service, in his seventh term in the House of Representatives, announced that he would retire at the end of his current term and not be a candidate for re-election. This threw the race wide open. Within a month eight candidates had announced their intention to run in the June primary, two Democrats and six Republicans.

Among the Republican candidates were a school principal, a schoolteacher, a member of the Riverside City Council, a retired navy admiral, and the scion of a highly respected pioneer family of landowners in Riverside County, a man named Fred Eldridge. The sixth candidate was the world-famous aviatrix Jacqueline Cochran Odlum, winner of many prizes in the field of aviation, leader of the women fliers during World War II, and wife of the multimillionaire financier, Floyd Odlum.

On the Democratic side were myself and a well-known Riverside County attorney, Mr. Carl Kegley, a man active in California politics who at one time had been a candidate for attorney general of the state of California on the Democratic ticket. . . .

Attempts to Disqualify Me

Before very long it was clear that the Republican race had narrowed itself down to Mrs. Odlum and Fred Eldridge, and throughout the period preceding the primary election I seemed to be the favorite on the Democratic side. But the primary campaign started to get extremely bitter in both the Democratic and Republican camps.

My Democratic opponent began efforts to have me disqualified as a candidate on the technical grounds that I had not been a citizen of the United States for seven years. According to the Constitution, a man has to be twenty-five years of age and a citizen for seven years before he can become a member of the House of Representatives. My opponent filed a petition, first in the Appellate Court and later in the Supreme Court of the state of California, asking for an injunction enjoining the county clerks of Riverside and Imperial counties from placing my name on the ballot. This gave me my first good break in the campaign.

I was by this time quite well known throughout Imperial County, but I was pretty much a complete stranger in so far as Riverside County was concerned. I doubt that when I announced my candidacy in November, 1955, I knew a hundred persons in Riverside County, and one of my big tasks was to make my name known there, and quickly. With more than 80 per cent of the registered voters of the entire 29th Congressional District, it was the main arena of the political contest.

Anyone familiar with a political campaign knows what value an issue such as the one my opponent raised is to a rival candidate who is completely unknown. When he filed suit against me, it became front-page, headline news in all the Riverside and Imperial County papers. Even if I could have afforded it, I couldn't have bought that kind of publicity.

I was thus not in the least disturbed by my opponent's move. Besides, I had familiarized myself thoroughly with the provisions of the Constitution and was positive that I was eligible to run. If elected in November, 1956, I would not take office until January, 1957, by which time I would have been a citizen of the United States seven years and sixteen days. . . .

As election time neared, my Democratic opponent became increasingly violent in his attacks on me. He quoted passages from my book, *My Mother, India*, quite out of context, and ran a virulent full-page ad in the newspapers of both counties. In addition he attacked me severely in several radio broadcasts. I paid little attention to these attacks, and in fact refused to listen to the radio broadcasts. Indeed, the full-page ad was of such a nature that the three leading daily papers in the district refused to print it on grounds that it was libelous. My friends were angry and disturbed over all this, but I couldn't let it bother me in the least. I had positively and definitely made up my mind to present myself as a candidate for the high office of congressman on my own merits and not say a word against my opponent. I thus never felt the need nor the desire to answer his charges.

Later in the general election the Republican campaign also hit hard at my being born in India. Every effort was made to make it appear that I was an Indian, not an American. In newspaper ads I was not called D. S. Saund, but Dalip Singh in big letters and Saund in small letters. This sort of practice was widespread, but apparently it did not hurt my candidacy either in the primary or general election.

In the primary election I won the Democratic nomination hands down with a tremendous majority. Mrs. Odlum won the Republican nomination only by a close margin from her runner up, Fred Eldridge, but she received a larger combined Republican and Democratic vote than I did. She was in the lead and thus started her campaign for the November general election with a fair assurance of victory. . . .

The Campaign

Our campaign attracted nationwide publicity. Mrs. Odlum was a national figure, a colorful personality with a Cinderella-like success story, while I was a native of India, seeking a high office no one of my race had ever held. *Time* magazine devoted a full-page article to the campaign in June, 1956; half of the page was devoted to my opponent and half to me. Newspapers all over the United States carried stories and national attention was focused on our particular congressional battle. This brought national figures of both political parties to the district. Vice President [Richard] Nixon came to Riverside to speak for Mrs. Odlum, while the highly popular governor of Tennessee, Frank Clement, the keynote speaker of the 1956 Democratic convention, gave a dramatic and eloquent endorsement of my candidacy before an overflow Democratic rally at Riverside. . . .

Although 1956 was a presidential election year as well as a year in which the state of California was to elect a new United States senator, the main interest of the voters of Riverside and Imperial counties was centered on the race for congressman of their district. This proved most helpful to me, since it made it that much easier for me to get a hearing. People everywhere were eager to meet me personally and learn my views on the issues in the campaign.

My opponent was positively opposed to any farm subsidy while I believed (and still do) that farmers need government protection in order to get a fair share in the economic rewards of our American life. I cited as an example the fact that while farmers constituted 18 per cent of the population in the United States, they received only 6 per cent of the total national income. I had farmed in Imperial County for twenty-five years and I was thoroughly acquainted with the problems in the Imperial, Coachella, and Palo Verde valleys, particularly in regard to their vital need for a continuous and controlled supply of water from the Colorado River. . . .

Achieving Victory

My opposition, as I have said, made an attempt to use my Indian origin against me. I decided to turn it to my own advantage and announced on a television broadcast that if elected I would immediately fly to India and the Far East. I would appear before the people there and tell them, "You have been listening to the insidious propaganda of the Communists that there is prejudice and discrimination in the United States against your people. Look, here I am. I am a living example of American democracy in action. I was elected by the free vote of the people in a very conservative district of the state of California to membership in the most powerful legislative body on the earth. Where else in the world could that happen?" . . .

The real climax of the campaign, however, was a debate between Mrs. Odlum and myself, held on Halloween night in a junior high-school auditorium in Riverside, just a few days before the election. The interest in the campaign was so great that long before the time of the meeting the auditorium was filled to capacity. The debate was broadcast over a network of radio stations in Riverside and Imperial counties. As at important political rallies and sports events, the broadcast started a half-hour before the debate began, and lasted nearly two hours. . . .

The debate reached a very large portion of the voters in Riverside and Imperial counties; some estimated that as many as forty to fifty thousand people heard it on radio. Furthermore, the entire debate, including the question-and-answer period, was reprinted in its entirety in the largest daily newspaper in the district, the Riverside *Press Enterprise*.

Mrs. Odlum had publicly challenged me to this debate and I must say it proved extremely helpful to me in my campaign. I could not possibly have reached that large an audience through any medium within the means of my campaign committee. She had big billboards throughout the area while I had the makeshift signs. She had the advantage of a well-organized campaign under the supervision of professional managers. I could not possibly match the lines of advertising in the newspapers or the professional quality of her ads. Almost all the press was emphatically on her side. Thus, reaching this great radio audience was a big help to me at the right time just a few days before the election.

After an exciting night of vote counting I came out on top—with a majority of 4,000 votes out of a total of 110,000 votes cast.

CHAPTER 3

COMING TO
AMERICA

A Third and Continuing Wave: Accomplishments and Challenges

East Indian Immigration Increases Due to the 1965 U.S. Immigration Act

David M. Reimers

East Indian immigration to the United States underwent a dramatic change as a result of the passage of the 1965 Immigration Act. The following selection by historian David M. Reimers describes the importance of that act and how it changed immigration in the United States. As Reimers writes, the 1965 legislation ended years of discrimination against third world immigrants by phasing out national origis quotas. Beginning in 1968, 170,000 visas were to be provided for people from the Eastern Hemisphere. Thousands of East Indian immigrants came to the United States to find better jobs, pursue higher learning, and reunite with family members, according to Reimers. Many of the East Indian immigrants of this period were "elites" such as doctors, engineers, and scientists. In the ensuing years East Indian immigrants began to branch out into other areas of the economy, becoming motel and restaurant owners, insurance agents, and realtors, for example.

Reimers is professor emeritus of history at New York University. His other books include Natives and Strangers: A Multicultural History of Americans *and* Unwelcome Strangers: American Identity and the Turn Against Immigration.

While European immigration shifted and then fell, that of Asia, the Caribbean basin, and South America rose significantly after 1965, and people from these third world areas accounted for about three-quarters of the four million immi-

David M. Reimers, *Still the Golden Door: The Third World Comes to America*. New York: Columbia University Press, 1992 pp, 92–116. Copyright © 1985, 1992, Columbia University Press, New York. All rights reserved. Republished with permission of the Columbia University Press, 61 W. 62nd St., New York, NY 10023.

grants of the 1970s, and the same pattern continued into the 1980s. By then Europeans amounted to only about 15 percent of the nation's latest immigrants, a dramatic change from historic patterns. In 1965 Asian immigrants totaled 20,683, about 5 percent of the total. By the late 1970s Asian immigration had increased sixfold and claimed over 40 percent of the newcomers. China, the Philippines, India, and Vietnam were among the leading nations sending people to America. In 1979 the seven leading exporters were all third world nations. The figures for 1980 revealed an even greater influx of third world people, for in that year over a quarter of a million refugees arrived from Vietnam, Cuba, and Haiti. By the late 1980s the top ten sending nations were from the third world. . . .

Why and how did Congress and the immigration reformers fail in 1965 to see the potential surge of Asian immigration? For one thing, they saw short queues for American visas in East Asian nations, at least when compared to the long queues in Italy or Greece, and they concluded that Asians lacked a strong desire to emigrate to the United States. Yet, these relatively short lines did not provide adequate indicators of future Asian immigration. Because most Asian nations had quotas of only 100 and because the Asia-Pacific Triangle had a ceiling of 2,000 until 1961, Asians felt discouraged about applying for visas to America. After all, if even a few thousand wanted to compete for one hundred places, the wait could be years. Of course some qualified as refugees or non-quota immigrants, but Asians clearly encountered difficulty emigrating to the United States before the amendments of 1965 ended their small quotas. . . .

Asians Apply for Visas

If the lines were short in Asia, applications for admission to the United States quickly grew when Congress passed the 1965 act, especially in the occupational preferences, and were a straw in the wind of things to come even before the new law was fully operative in July 1968. In early January 1968 [Philip M. Boffey,] a reporter for *Science* wrote, "A handful of American officials has been aware for several months that a dramatic shift in the composition of the brain drain was likely, but this realization did not reach a wider public until the State Department's Visa Office published a detailed analysis of the new law late in November." The writer was referring to the many Asians applying for visas as the new law became effective. Whereas under the old system scientists from Germany or Great Britain could almost immigrate at will, now they were on a first-come, first-served basis in entering under the third preference for professionals. By July 1968 the backlog had reached 48,000 for that preference's 17,000 annual places (including family members). India, China, Korea, and the Philippines claimed the most persons on the waiting lists. Europeans had lost their advantages and now those who wanted to emigrate to America had to wait their turn.

If short lines before 1965 fooled the politicians, so did the new law's family preference system's potential for chain migration.[1] The 1965 amendments emphasized family unification and because the Asian-American population was less than 1 percent of the American total in 1960, few believed that Asians possessed the necessary kinship networks for immigration. As noted, groups diverse as the Japanese American Citizens League and the American Legion predicted that the family unification system would keep immigration moving along its prior nationality paths. Politicians and reformers did not see how few persons were required for a network under the family preferences of the 1965 act. This new immigration can be seen by the following hypothetical example. Not untypically, and unforeseen by the 1965 reformers, an Asian student comes to America as a nonimmigrant to complete his education. While finishing his studies, he finds a job, gets Labor Depart-

---

1. In chain migration, one immigrant sponsors several other immigrants, who then sponsor several others themselves.

ment certification, and becomes an immigrant. Once an immigrant he uses the second preference to bring over his spouse and children. A few years later the new immigrant, and his spouse, become citizens and are eligible to sponsor their brothers and sisters under the fifth, the largest and most popular preference, or to bring in their nonquota parents. Needless to say, the brothers and sisters, once immigrants, can also use the second preference to bring in their spouses and children and expand the immigrant kin network still further when they become citizens. No wonder the 1965 law came to be called the brothers and sisters act. . . .

Incentives for Emigration

Because Congress conceived of family unification as a conservative change and because Asians lacked long lines for visas both critics and defenders of the new system generally underestimated the impact of the law on third world immigration. Yet, other signs, unclear in the early 1960s, pointed to a potential surge of Asian immigration to the United States.

In the first place, American wages and the standard of living were considerably higher than throughout Asia. Japan, of course, grew at a rapid rate after 1960 and could hardly be considered a developing third world nation; hence, Japanese immigration remained relatively low, and remained at the same level after 1965. Most other Asian nations experienced poverty, hunger, and deprivation. Yet, even the elites had incentives for emigration. Among the educated middle classes, in India, the Philippines, and Korea, people found that they possessed educations and skills not in demand in their nations, or that wages and working conditions were better in America. Moreover, unstable political and social conditions prompted uneasiness among some about the future.

Immigration is more than simply economics—low wages, low per capita income, poverty—or high birthrates or political instability. Knowledge is another important factor. In the nineteenth century, railroads, steamship lines, and state bureaus of immigration promoted emigration from Europe to America by providing Europeans with information. In addition, letters from those who had already gone told families and friends in the Old World about the wonders of the new. In the past, these letters contained money to bring their countrymen to America. In the period after World War II information about America has become more plentiful than ever before and has penetrated deeply into the third world nations. . . .

The Role of Students

If modern communications brought the news of the good life, modern transportation made it possible. The airplane has become for Asians what the fast steamship line was to the nineteenth-century Europeans. While the media often gave the first impressions of America, actual contact, due to easy and relatively inexpensive travel, reinforced them. In 1978 exclusive of Canadians and Mexicans, over nine million people entered the United States as nonimmigrants—students, visitors, business people—most of whom arrived by air. This figure represented a fourfold increase over the early 1960s. Thousands of Asians studied in the United States after 1960. Before the enactment of the 1965 reforms, about 50,000 foreign students annually attended American universities, but by 1981 this figure had reached approximately 300,000: Asians accounted for nearly half the total. The vast majority of foreign students returned after completing their education here, but some adjusted their status to resident aliens by marrying Americans or taking jobs in the United States. In 1978 over 18,000 nonimmigrant students became immigrants; of these about two-thirds were Asians. . . .

Medical Immigrants

Asians with professional training entered to work in a variety of fields, but none caught the public eye so much as the physicians and other medical professionals. Changes in the structure of medical service in the United States combined with the 1965 Immigration Act to increase substantially these third world medical immigrants. From the end of World War II to 1965, American medical schools graduated an almost constant number of physicians. They were inadequate to satisfy the demand and many hospitals looked abroad for their staffs. About 15,000 foreign doctors entered during the 1950s. This brain drain was predominately composed of Europeans and Canadians, with some increase in the proportion of doctors from Latin America and Asia in the early 1960s. Beginning in the 1960s the federal government encouraged with financial aid an increase in the American supply. By 1974, 121 medical schools enrolled 53,554 students compared to 35,833 in 91 schools in 1968. Yet this increase was not enough; hence, hospitals still looked abroad and Asian physicians filled the need. In part, the demand was high because of population growth and America's willingness to pay for more medical care. But also important was the expansion of medical services due to federal government programs. The same year that Congress changed the immigration law, 1965, it also passed Medicare and Medicaid, which created an enlarged demand for medical services, especially in the inner city hospitals. Growing private health insurance plans also stimulated a need for more medical services.

In the years 1965–1974, 75,000 foreign physicians entered the United States either to work temporarily or to practice medicine on a permanent basis. By 1974 foreign physicians made up one fifth of the total physicians in the United States and one third of the interns and residents. In some cities they were a higher proportion of interns. In New York City in the mid-1970s, Asian immigrant doctors made up more than half of the interns of the municipal hospitals, and 80 percent at voluntary hospitals like Brooklyn Hospital. . . .

In 1976 the medical profession persuaded Congress to cut back on the supply of foreign physicians, to limit them to training and research positions. Yet urban hospitals still experienced shortages of both doctors and nurses, and the rules were modified in 1981. In 1987, the regulations were tightened again, but at that time about 15 percent of American physicians were foreign born and 22 percent foreign educated. . . .

Asian medical professionals generally settled in states where large cities, such as New York, Chicago, and Los Angeles, needed their services. Like other immigrants they often took less desirable jobs. In the case of doctors and nurses, this meant in inner city hospitals serving the poor, blacks, Hispanics, and the aged, or in rural areas where doctors were in demand, or they practiced in the lower-paid specialties of their occupation. Some had difficulty in passing state English language requirements or meeting residency or citizenship requirements. Yet in spite of these difficulties, American medical practice continued to attract Asians. . . .

East Indian Immigrants

Among Asians, East Indians trailed Filipinos, Chinese, and Koreans in numbers. Like the Koreans, few Indians had emigrated to the United States before 1950. Not many possessed the necessary family contacts in 1965 to take immediate advantage of the new law. Moreover, the United States did not have military forces stationed in India; hence, few "war brides" came from that country. Yet, India increased its immigration substantially. In the ten years after 1965, the figures topped 115,000. In 1976 immigration from India passed 17,000; in 1977 it went over 18,000 and in 1978 it was over 20,000. It topped 22,000 in 1980. India was becoming one of the largest source nations for American immigration.

The first Indian immigrants entering after 1965 were predominately males who took jobs in American urban hospitals, universities, or businesses eager to employ their skills. Next to

Filipinos and Koreans, Indians made up the largest contingent of East Asian medical professionals, including nurses and physicians.

Not all of the Indian professionals were physicians. They also included scientists and engineers. In 1978 the National Science Foundation reported that Asia accounted for slightly more than half of the immigrant scientists and engineers of that year. India had the largest number of any nation and accounted for one third of the Asian total. Mostly these were engineers.

These immigrants found that their Westernized education in India, or sometimes in the United States, did not necessarily lead to suitable employment. Like the doctor immigrants, they found conditions in the United States to be more attractive than at home. In any event, the Indian migration was truly an elite group. In 1975 immigration authorities classified the vast majority of Indian immigrants as professional/technical workers or their immediate families, a higher rate than for any other nation. Of those Indians claiming an occupation, nearly three quarters were professionals, technical, and kindred workers or managers or administrators.

Developing in the Business Community

As the elite settled and began to bring their families and as more Indians began to use family preferences, the social base of immigrants broadened, the sex ratio of immigrants narrowed slightly, and Indian communities developed, notably in New York City. These communities included Hindu, Hare Krishna, and Gita temples and a number of social and cultural organizations. In August 1981, New York Indians decided to celebrate their ethnicity in a traditional American way. "We realized that it was time we started having a parade like other ethnic communities," said a spokesman for the Federation of India Association [in the August 17, 1981, *New York Times*]. In New York City style, the mayor proclaimed an India Day to mark the procession, which featured eighteen floats. Said New York City's then mayor, Ed Koch, "They are hard working and devoted to this city and this country. They give us their culture and their taxes—and their wonderful restaurants."

Koch may have had in mind the businesses begun by one family, originally from Bangladesh, responsible for opening several restaurants on Manhattan's Sixth Street. Beginning in 1968, several brothers, some of whom originally came as students, opened an Indian restaurant along that street. Within several years, the brothers opened several more and when a brother-in-law and former waiter wanted to have his own restaurant, they assisted him. Later an uncle started another restaurant. These small eating places attracted still others so that by 1981 ten were open for business, giving that street a reputation as "Little India."

In addition to restaurants, Indians also purchased many motels, at first in California and then across the country. By 1989 Indians were estimated to own 40 percent of the nation's smaller motels (those with fewer than 56 rooms), and Days Inns of America reported that one quarter of its franchises were operated by Indians. Most Indian motel owners were from the western Indian state of Gujarat, with a large number carrying the common name of Patel. Motels required more capital than the greengroceries run by Koreans, but many of the Indians were from the elite classes or had made money first in Africa (Uganda) and Britain. One newly naturalized citizen, Ratan Patel of Michigan, combined engineering with business. An engineer for the Ford Motor company, he bought the Maple Lawn Motel near Detroit for his wife and brother-in-law to run, while he worked full time at Ford. Asian Indians also branched out from motels. In the 1980s some began selling insurance, while others were venturing into real estate.

The Struggle to Succeed in America

S. Mitra Kalita

Many East Indian immigrants who moved to the United States after the passage of the 1965 Immigration Act were lured by the expectation of good jobs, high wages, and career advancement. Some had their dreams of scholarships, grants, or promotions fulfilled. But for others the reality was often very different from their dreams. Even immigrants with professional backgrounds were often unable to step into jobs similar to the ones they held in India. Like former bank manager Harish Patel, who came to the United States in 1990, they had to take any job to survive. As author S. Mitra Kalita describes in this selection, the endless hours of hard work at odd jobs discouraged Patel and pushed him to return to his homeland. Once at home, however, the pull of better opportunities in the United States and the urgings of his daughter made him reconsider his decision. Patel moved back to the United States to try his luck again. Over the years, he moved back and forth between the United States and India several times. Patel's story is an example of the difficulties some immigrants have in launching their new lives in a new country, Kalita writes. Despite the challenges in finding work, Patel and his family remained in the United States.

Kalita is a second-generation Indian American. She reports on business for the Washington Post. *She is the author of* Suburban Sahibs: Three Immigrant Families and Their Passage from India to America, *from which this selection is excerpted.*

Harish Patel's eyes fixed on the door exiting customs at John F. Kennedy International Airport. For almost two years, the forty-three-year-old had started his day at 8:00 A.M.

S. Mitra Kalita, *Suburban Sahibs: Three Immigrant Families and Their Passage from India to America.* New Brunswick, NJ: Rutgers University Press, 2003, pp. 47–51. Copyright © 2003 by S. Mitra Kalita. All rights reserved. Reprinted by permission of Rutgers University Press.

as a factory worker and ended it at midnight as a security guard to earn and save enough money for his wife and two daughters to join him. Their arrival would make the family whole again, Harish thought. And what a day they had picked to begin life in America. It was July 3, 1990. His daughters would surely find the next day's fireworks display near Harish's apartment in Edison [New Jersey] reminiscent of those put on for their new year of Diwali.

Harish looked up when he heard the automatic doors open. Indians, some clad in saris, others in jeans and T-shirts, started to exit. Finally, Harish caught sight of his wife, Kapila, pushing a cart of suitcases, hand luggage, and shopping bags. She was wearing a salwar kameez [loose pants and shirt worn by some women in India and by both men and women in Pakistan and Afghanistan]. Behind her came the girls, Zankhana and Kajal, ages fifteen and eight.

Harish went to them and touched Kapila's arm. He patted Kajal on the head and assessed how much she had grown. Addressing her with the Gujarati [the language of Gujarat, a state in western India] word for daughter, he said: "Beti, do you remember me?"

Kajal looked up at Harish. "No," she said. "I don't."

He couldn't blame her. Since Kajal was a toddler Harish had been flying back and forth between the United States and India. He had lived in Detroit; Durham, North Carolina; Hollywood, California; Lowell, Massachusetts; and three places in New Jersey—Jersey City, the Fords section of Woodbridge, and finally Edison. None had ever felt like home. In Harish's mind, home would only be one place: his simple two-bedroom house near close friends and extended family in Baroda. Back home, Harish Patel had worked as a supervisor in the foreign-exchange division of the Bank of Baroda. He started in 1970 as a teller, earning 250 rupees [the currency of India] per month, and worked his way up to management. As a manager, he was able to sign cash-withdrawal forms and those who reported to him called him "sir." When Harish left the bank for good, his salary was 5,500 rupees a month, at the time more than most Indians made in a year.

Working in America

Among his jobs in the United States, he pumped gas, packed boxes, filled pill bottles rolling off an assembly line, watched for shoplifters as a security guard, and sold newspapers. His two brothers who had preceded him to the States never told him of the hardship that came with living there. Instead, their stories of America—the cars, the jeans, the money—impressed Harish Patel enough to lure him away from home. Since then, Harish had spent every day in America convincing himself the greater opportunity, especially the chance for his daughters to get a good education, was worth turning his back on home.

Harish Patel was born the same year that India won its independence from the British, 1947. He benefited from one of the remnants of British colonial rule, namely, an English education. When Harish was a boy, his parents were among the millions of Indians who left their villages for opportunities in the city. The grandsons of a bullock farmer and sons of a civil engineer, Harish and his four brothers were taught to value education and professional types of work. He became a banker after earning his bachelor's degree in economics from the University of Ahmedabad, a city about 110 miles from Baroda. On May 21, 1970, at the age of twenty-three, he wed Kapila, then eighteen, in a marriage arranged one month before. In the 1970s, two of Harish's brothers emigrated from Gujarat to the United States. One found work as a civil engineer in Detroit; the other was admitted to Duke University in Durham, North Carolina, for a Ph.D. program. The brothers returned to India every three or four years; each time, they bestowed gifts of dolls and dresses upon Harish's daughters and impressed everyone with the value of their dollar once converted

to the Indian rupee. *American money can be spent like water,*
Harish observed.

His elder daughter, Zankhana, wanted her father to be a
part of that lifestyle. "Papa, why don't you go to America?" she
repeatedly asked. Harish saw no reason not to try, so he agreed
to allow his eldest brother, Arvind, to sponsor him on an immigration status that would eventually lead to a green card.

On March 20, 1985, carrying a one-way ticket and $20,
Harish landed in America. He arrived in a nation whose dollar was steadily falling; on the day Harish's plane touched
down, newspapers nationwide reported that consumer confidence suffered the worst drop in twenty years after the closure
of seventy private savings and loan institutions.

Harish flew to Detroit to join Arvind, a civil engineer. For
a week, Harish tried to find work, searching through classified
ads every morning. He soon gave up and asked Arvind to lend
him money to return home, since he was officially on a leave
from his banking job. His brother refused and resorted to
tough love: "If you want to go back, you'll have to get a job
and make the money on your own."

Harish then went to Durham to stay with his younger
brother Indravadan, who helped him find a maintenance job
at a restaurant, collecting trash, sweeping the sidewalks, and
watering the landscaping for $3.25 per hour. After four days
of performing work Harish felt was beneath him, he decided
to try his luck in New York City at the urging of family friends
who lived in Queens. Two weeks of searching for a job produced nothing, so he called an old friend of his father's in Jersey City who owned a candy store. The storeowner agreed to
pay Harish $3 per hour as a guard. Harish was specifically
told to "watch the . . . people who try to steal." That job ended
when Harish started to fear the people he was told to watch
and reprimand. . . . At about five-foot-seven and 180 pounds,
Harish is not a slight man, but he thought no amount of
weight could save him from the guns the storeowner told him
thieves and shoplifters carried.

Home and Then Back to America

Already in debt to his brothers and the family friends who had been housing him and giving him pocket money, Harish panicked at the thought of spending any more time in the United States. He stopped smoking cigarettes because he could no longer afford them. Finally, Harish landed a job at an Emerson Radio warehouse in North Bergen, New Jersey, as a material handler. For $4.25 per hour, he took television sets off the assembly line and loaded them into boxes lined with Styrofoam. For four months, he worked ten-hour days, taking hot baths in his friend's Jersey City apartment to soothe his aching back.

With each paycheck, Harish counted down from $600, the price of an airline ticket. By October, he had saved $457. Harish couldn't wait any longer to get home. He called his brother in North Carolina and successfully begged for $150 so he could buy a ticket to Bombay. Just before he left, Harish Patel received his green card, ensuring he could return to the United States as one of its permanent residents.

Harish slipped back into his old job at the Bank of Baroda. He resumed smoking. Unlike his brothers, who raved about America's virtues upon their returns to India, Harish reported to everyone he met that America was an awful, lonely, backbreaking place to live and work. "Don't go, don't go," he told whomever he could.

Still, in May 1987, when a friend called him and told him he could use some help running his motel in Hollywood, California, Harish returned. Here was a chance to try America again with a job in hand. Besides, Harish reasoned, he had to return to America within two years after his green card was issued or face its revocation. Harish once again found a weakening U.S. economy. Inflation and gas prices were up, stock markets volatile.

The motel was in a [bad] section of town . . . and he was scared once again. When he overheard his friend's wife complaining about Harish living in the motel for free, Harish knew it was time to return to Gujarat. He had not lasted in America even twenty-five days.

He did not last in Baroda for much longer. In the fall of 1988, Harish couldn't ignore the differences between India and America anymore. In India, government officials were corrupt and accepted, even demanded, bribes for routine services. Luckily, Zankhana and Kajal were able to attend the school of their choice without the Patels having to pay a bribe, but Harish heard from neighbors and relatives that such bribes were becoming the norm. *How long can my family last in India?* Harish vowed to try America once more, despite now familiar reports of its economy softening. Once again, Harish returned to the United States, this time to Lowell, Massachusetts, to stay with a distant relative of his in-laws.

Sajjan Bhagat knew of Harish's futility and frustration in the United States and vowed things would be different this time. As soon as Harish awoke the morning after his arrival, Sajjan took him to a job he had already found for his friend as a security guard in an office complex. To pay off the money Harish had borrowed from his brothers and friends, he worked sixteen-hour days from 4:00 P.M. until 8:00 A.M. Sajjan taught him how to drive: Harish obtained his driver's license and bought a used car. He found himself happy for the first time in America. But after five months, Harish received a phone call from his younger brother. "Harish, you're a banker," Jyotindra said. "Why are you working as a security guard?" . . . Harish said he would move south for better opportunities.

Harish sold his car, returned to New Jersey, and moved into an apartment in Jersey City with his brother. He quickly found work on a pharmaceutical company's assembly line. For his job readying bottles of ibuprofen for shipping, Harish stuck the label on the bottle, waited for one hundred capsules to be dropped into its open mouth—he had to count them himself—and capped the bottle before the next filling, seconds later. Sometimes, if he was too slow or the machine too fast, the pills would spill across the counter and Harish would have to start the count to one hundred all over again. To Harish, the job didn't feel like a step up from a security guard. So after three months, when his supervisor at the Bank of Baroda sent word that he had to return or face termination, Harish happily went home.

"You're Not Trying Hard Enough"

By the winter of 1988, Harish had been back and forth between the United States and Baroda three times in as many years. That winter, the New Jersey Senate passed a $16.5 million aid package to help the state's thousands of unemployed residents. New Jersey governor Tom Kean imposed a hiring freeze. AT&T laid off 16,000 workers. Yet an ocean away in India, Harish's daughter Zankhana, then thirteen, couldn't understand why he wasn't making it like her uncles had. "You're just not trying hard enough, Papa," she said. "Next time when you go, you can't come back. We'll come to you."

Harish didn't bother explaining to her that he had been competing with thousands of the native-born unemployed for work or that banks had already told him he had little chance succeeding in America. "Your systems in India are different from ours," they would say. They were right. In Indian banks, each teller was given a different task, authorizing withdrawals or deposits or check cashing, but never all at the same time. It would be more than a decade until most Indian banks were computerized; instead, each account number and signature had to be authorized from a registry of books kept in stacks behind the tellers' desks. The first computers Harish ever saw were in America. Not only did the Indian system employ workers who never learned all aspects of running a bank, but it also made for long lines and impatient customers. Even as the twenty-first century began, the Bank of Baroda's main room remained separated into lines under signs that said Remittances, Saving Bank Accounts, Current Accounts, Over-drafts, Cash Receipts, Cash Payments. Harish was almost tempted to agree with the banks that told him he had no chance, except that he felt most comfortable and respectable as a banker. Those other jobs would be just something he'd endure until the right opportunity came along.

Harish thought about trying to get white-collar work in clerical, bookkeeping, or accounting positions, but those jobs seemed to require English skills he didn't have. His English was perfectly understandable, but when interviewers started talking fast, he tended to get easily confused and lost in the conversation. If he didn't understand a concept, he pretended not to understand the English. For years after immigrating, Harish could not conduct an extensive phone conversation in English. He did not tell his daughters and Kapila, who were living off the family's savings, that employers told him he was "hard to understand" or had "too heavy an accent."

In the spring of 1989, Harish Patel returned to the United States with his daughter's words echoing throughout the eighteen-hour plane ride between Bombay and JFK International.

East Indians Retain Their Culinary Traditions in New York

Madhulika S. Khandelwal

The borough of Queens in New York City has the largest urban population of Indian immigrants in the United States. Indian immigrants have been arriving in Queens since the 1965 Immigration Act removed national origin quotas and allowed up to twenty thousand immigrants from each country in the Eastern Hemisphere to come to the United States each year. By the 1990s Queens contained hundreds of Indian-owned businesses. In the following excerpt from her book Becoming American, Being Indian, *author Madhulika S. Khandelwal describes the East Indian community in Queens, where people can buy the ingredients for their regional cuisines, rent a video of an Indian film, buy an Indian newspaper or magazine, and learn about East Indian cultural events. Khandelwal also describes many of the Indian specialties and Indian American innovations available in Queens, including vegetarian pizza and frozen samosas (fried dumplings).*

Khandelwal was born in India and educated there and in the United States. She is a professor of urban studies at Queens College, City University of New York.

Preserving cultural tradition has marked Indian immigrant activities continuously since the 1960s, but a distinct pattern is discernible from the mid-1970s through the 1990s. By the later period, many Indian cultures could be identified in Queens, each oriented to a distinct regional, class, religious, and generational clientele. Though based in this borough,

Madhulika S. Khandelwal, *Becoming American, Being Indian: An Immigrant Community in New York City.* Ithaca, NY: Cornell University Press, 2002, pp. 36–43. Copyright © 2002 by Cornell University Press. Used by permission of the publisher, Cornell University Press.

these activities drew upon networks extending to elsewhere in the city and its suburbs, and to other parts of the country, overseas Indian communities, and India. This busy calendar of Indian cultural activities, most of them concentrated in Queens, thus linked New York to a worldwide chain of Indian diasporic [immigrant] centers in London, Toronto, Guyana, and elsewhere. . . .

Traditions Related to Food

Indian immigrants brought their food-related traditions to New York. They were often heard defining their culture in terms of their regional or religious foodways: "In our culture, we eat [a particular dish]" or "In our community, food is prepared [in a particular way]." Indian parents expected their U.S.-reared children to appreciate home-cooked food more than a meal eaten out. One young Indian American complained that her mother wanted her to eat at home in the morning before leaving for the day. "Every day she persuades me to have breakfast at home. And here I am, busy getting ready for school. I would rather stop somewhere on my way for coffee. I don't know why she wants me to sit at the dining table and eat her home-prepared breakfast." Her mother responded, "I don't understand the sense in spending money outside when there is food at home. On one hand, she says continuously that she doesn't have money, and then she throws money away like this. This reason of saving time is a mere excuse. Do you think she will save time by buying breakfast from outside? It's so American to drink and eat while you are driving." Despite such disagreements, most young Indian Americans were well aware of their mothers' cooking talents and asked them to prepare Indian meals on special occasions.

A large part of India's people live their entire lives without tasting animal products (including, for most, eggs); many who are not vegetarians eat meat only outside the home. Vegetarianism is so widespread in India that any large gathering or restaurant may serve only vegetarian food or may carry separate sections of food for vegetarians and nonvegetarians. Indian vegetarianism is associated with Hinduism, although the religion does not require such a practice and although many Hindus do consume nonvegetarian food. Traditional Indian philosophy, however, laid out rules of nutrition that emphasized vegetarian foods for both spiritual and physical well-being. It is therefore common for even nonvegetarian Hindus to practice vegetarianism on certain religious days in the Hindu calendar. Meat items, even eggs, cannot enter most Hindu kitchens, and most restaurants in India are solely vegetarian.

Although some Hindu immigrants in the United States have abandoned pure vegetarianism, many others conform to tradition. Some immigrants who have become more religious here are also dedicated vegetarians. . . .

In a number of pan-Asian organizational events in New York City, Indians regularly refrained from refreshments or meals that had any nonvegetarian ingredients, including sauces and broths. In some instances this practice was both an inconvenience to the vegetarian Indian and embarrassing to the host. Often, awkward situations also arose on trips, although domestic and international airplane flights more easily provided the option of requesting a vegetarian special meal. Still according to one Indian immigrant woman, maintaining vegetarianism was not particularly difficult in New York. "There is such a large variety of foods available here. There are salads, pastas, breads, Middle Eastern food, and, then of course, we have pizzas. It *is* more difficult to be eating out a lot when you are a vegetarian, but it is easy with home cooking. Now almost every ingredient necessary for Indian cooking is available in New York, thanks to the grocery stores. Even the quality of spices and other packaged foods that we get here is better than what we get in India."

The Growth of Indian Food Stores

Before the establishment of Indian stores in Queens in the early 1970s, Indian immigrants had to make do with American grocery stores or travel to Kalustyan's, on Lexington Avenue in Manhattan. House of Spices, the first Indian grocery in Queens, opened in Elmhurst in 1970, and as the Indian population grew, other stores appeared in Flushing and later in Jackson Heights. Indians from beyond New York combined visits to the city with shopping at these stores, purchasing bulk supplies of basmati rice and Indian vegetables not available at their local Indian grocery, or not at New York prices. The retail food businesses in Queens eventually became quite competitive, and stores offered a fuller range of ethnic ingredients to their Indian customers. By the 1980s "Indo-Pak-Bangla" stores carried an array of spices, lentils, flours, sweets, snacks, fresh vegetables, cans and jars of spicy pickles, frozen items, and prepared packaged foods. The variety variable in each category also increased. To the delight of Indian customers, stores carried mustard greens and fresh fenugreek in their produce sections, and cases of mangoes imported from Mexico, Haiti, or Florida during the summer. Perplexingly to the occasional American customer, these stores contained only limited offerings of Indian curry powder. One store owner explained: "You ask any Indian, and they don't even know what curry powder is. Instead, every Indian kitchen carries a range of spices that are used differently according to the dishes. Curry powder is for Americans who do not know how to prepare Indian food. They want a short cut so that they do not have to buy different spices and learn their uses."

To maximize their business, groceries in Queens also carried videocassettes of Indian movies for rental, and ritual items for upcoming festivals. They also served as information exchange centers. Their walls were plastered with large colored posters of concerts and other cultural events, often with tickets available right there, and they sold Indian newspapers and magazines and made space available for flyers announcing job openings and real estate offerings. . . .

The influence of immigrant life in America was also obvious in these stores. A single grocery carried a wider range of cooking pastes and powders—for Gujarati, Punjabi, South Indian, and other cuisines—than would be available in a single store in any part of India. Out of commercial necessity, grocery stores were perhaps the most powerful promoters of pan-Indian and pan-South Asian unity; a jar of pickles or a bag of rice might be used by immigrants from India, Bangladesh, Pakistan, or Sri Lanka. And in response to the fast pace of American life, each store had a frozen-food section of packets of green peas, fried onions, chunks of *paneer* (cheese usually prepared at home in India), precooked *samosas* (fried patties with potato filling), *chapatis* and *parathas* (Indian breads), and other items. A store owner in Flushing exclaimed, "I have been in this country for many years, but I have not seen a group like us Indians where women prepare their bread every day from scratch. They work [outside the home] here and have no help in cooking and cleaning. The frozen foods are for this sector of Indian customers." Frozen foods were also convenient for single men who cooked for themselves, something they were not trained to do in India. . . .

Eating Out in Restaurants

The Indian restaurants that opened in Queens after the 1970s, unlike those in Manhattan, served a primarily Indian clientele. The cluster located on 74th Street in Jackson Heights included the Jackson Diner, which replaced an American diner and served Indian cuisine. By the late 1980s similar restaurants had appeared all over Queens and Long Island. In its inaugural publicity one restaurant, Tandoor in Rego Park, described Queens as the "capital of Indians in America." These mid- to upscale restaurants based their trade on well-to-do customers, largely Indian, who, besides dining, hired restaurant space for weddings, birthdays, or parties. Patrons were not primarily residents of the neighborhood, but came from far and near.

Simultaneously a number of inexpensive eating places cropped up in the Queens neighborhoods receiving newly arrived immigrants. Their clientele (and workforce) were recent immigrants, including lower-middle- to working-class Indians, Bangladeshis, and Pakistanis. Meals were of the fast-food variety, with customers choosing from a limited range displayed in steam tables. . . . These "curry in a hurry" eateries carried both vegetarian and nonvegetarian items, cooked according to a standardized North Indian style that appealed as well to Pakistanis and Bangladeshis. . . .

Among all New York Indians, the food next in popularity to their own was pizza, which also suited the vegetarian preference of many immigrants. Indian families patronized the Pizza Hut chain, but the first notable indication of the popularity of pizza was the large Indian clientele of a restaurant in Elmhurst called Singa's Pizza. This Greek-owned pizzeria, opened in 1967, sold a small eight-inch pie with various meat and vegetable toppings (including hot pepper) and became a favorite among Indian immigrants. Pizza was preferred as an inexpensive alternative to family dining in Indian restaurants and a timesaver versus cooking at home. Indian families who did not live in Queens made sure to pick up pizzas from Singa's when visiting the borough. Spurred by its popularity among Indians, Singa's opened other outlets in Flushing and Long Island City, neighborhoods with large Indian populations; its opening in Flushing in the early 1990s was publicized in the Indian ethnic press. In the mid-1990s other pizzerias in Queens tried to succeed by using names similar to Singa's, but as one Indian customer explained, "We miss its special taste. I cannot say exactly why we like it so much, but somehow it has clicked with the Indian palate. Where else would you get such wonderful hot chili topping, and mango drink, to go with a pizza?"

East Indians Establish a Political Identity

Vinay Lal

The majority of the East Indian immigrants living in the United States arrived as a result of the 1965 Immigration Act. This landmark legislation eliminated national origin quotas for immigrants and marked the beginning of an influx of people from Asia, the Caribbean, and Latin America. In the following selection, author Vinay Lal describes the growth of the East Indian community in the United States and its developing political awareness and involvement. In the 1980s, Lal writes, East Indians created many strong professional organizations in order to combat discrimination and lobby Congress. Organizing as a group for the purpose of bringing about change is something East Indians have learned to do quite well in their adopted land, Lal points out, but he argues that too many Indian Americans still allow political events in India to influence their behaviors in the United States. He also argues that too few East Indians seek high political office in America.

Lal is associate professor of history at the University of California at Los Angeles. His published works include Empire of Knowledge *and* Of Cricket, Guiness and Gandhi: Essays on Indian History and Culture.

The most contemporary phase of the political history of Asian Indians in the United States begins ... with the Immigration and Naturalization Act of 1965, which set a quota of 20,000 immigrants from each country. The greater number of Indians, at least in the first fifteen years, were to arrive as

Vinay Lal, "Establishing Roots, Engendering Awareness: A Political History of Asian Indians in the United States," in *Live Like the Banyan Tree: Images of the Indian American Experience*, edited by Leela Prasad. Philadelphia: The Balch Institute Collections, The Historical Society of Pennsylvania, 1999, pp. 42–48. Reproduced by permission of the Historical Society of Pennsylvania (HSP).

professionals, though subsequently many more have come under family reunification preferential categories. By 1975 the
number of Asian Indians had risen to well over 175,000, and
it is around this time that the question of self-representation,
and how they wished to be known collectively to others, first
surfaced among members of the Indian community. One
American scholar who published in 1980 a study of Asian Indians in New York City reported that her informants variously
described themselves as Aryan, Indo-Aryan, Caucasian, Oriental, Indian, Asian, Mongol, and Dravidian. The earlier nomen-
clature of "Hindus" for all Indians had long been abandoned,
but their designation as "Indians" was scarcely more acceptable, since what are now known as "Native Americans" were
also known as "Indians". The term "Asian American" was not
much in vogue, and in any case referred primarily to those
from the Far East (and later South-east Asia); and unlike in
Britain, where Indians appeared to tolerate being lumped together with Africans and Caribbean people as "black", even
deriving new political coalitions and formations in the common interest of combating oppression, in the United States
the designation "black" was seen as condemning one to membership in a permanent underclass.

The aversion of Indians to being viewed as part of a
"black" community no doubt owes something also to their
own racism. . . . To be assimilated into the category of "Caucasian" or "white" might consequently seem desirable, but Indians could not then claim those entitlements due to members of "minority groups" that faced the real hazards of
prejudice. Where, at one time, Indians were zealous in press-
ing forth the claim that they ought to be considered "white",
they now sought to disassociate themselves from this identity
without disavowing the category of "Caucasian", which was
seen as prestigious and having scientific credibility. . . .

The Classification of "Asian Indian" Is Born

These efforts at preserving the minority status of Indians,
while allowing them a distinct identity, were to bear fruit

when the Census Bureau agreed to reclassify immigrants from India as "Asian Indians". . . . There was something of a case to be made for disadvantages suffered by Indians, for as the 1980 census showed, U.S.-born Asian Indians, whose numbers were growing, had an unemployment rate "five times that of other Asian American groups." Moreover, though among Indians there were proportionately more professionals than among any other ethnic group, with every passing year the number of Indians employed as taxi drivers, gas station owners and attendants, subway newsagent vendors, and in other working-class jobs would continue to grow, and the apprehension that these Asian Indians might have to bear the brunt of racial prejudice and ethnic jokes, whether at work or at home, was not entirely misplaced. In the late 1980s, this racism, which had taken a violent turn on previous occasions, acquired a systematic patterning. In New Jersey, for instance, a number of Indians, whose material success rendered them visibly open to attack, were murdered by young white men who came to be known as "dot busters", a reference to the *bindi* or colored dot placed by some Hindu women on their forehead between the eyebrows.

Organizing to Protect Indian Interests

Among Indian professionals, likewise, there was the sense that the discrimination that has characteristically been encountered by every immigrant group for a generation or two might also stare them in the face. This feeling began to acquire some urgency in the early 1980s and was the impetus for a formation of a number of important professional organizations. As the laws governing the admission of doctors from overseas into the American medical profession were tightened, the American Association of Physicians from India (AAPI) was formed to represent this constituency. According to an estimate furnished in 1993, Indian doctors comprised an extraordinary 4 percent of their profession, and the high profile of AAPI can be gauged by the fact that its annual convention in 1995 was addressed by President [Bill] Clinton. Other broader-based organizations also emerged to enhance and safeguard Indian interests: prominent among these, other than the AIA (Association of Indians in America), are the Federation of Indian American Associations (FIA), the National Federation of Indian American Associations (NFIA), and the National Association of Americans of Asian Indian Descent (NAAAID). The NFIA, together with the American Indian Forum for Political Education and AAPI, agitated against proposed legislation in 1985 that would have deeply cut Medicare funding to hospitals employing doctors with foreign medical degrees. The NFIA was also to show the way in how Asian Indians might further the interests of the Indian nation-state, when in 1987 it mobilized the Indian community, with apparent success, to persuade Congress to withdraw the sale of sophisticated AWACS planes [that contain high-tech surveillance and communication systems] to Pakistan....

Lobbying at the Local Level

It is at the local level that Indian community activists and organizations have done some of their most intense lobbying, not always successfully. The Little India Chamber of Commerce, in the partly Indian neighborhood of Artesia outside Los Angeles, has been unable to persuade the municipality to put up signs guiding visitors to "Little India". Here, as in New York and Chicago, Indian businesses have been charged with lacking political acumen and cultural sensitivity, as apparently evidenced by their refusal to keep shops closed on the Fourth of July. Most often, however, the lobbying takes the form of attempts to have 'great' Indians memorialized. A school has been named after Mahatma Gandhi in Jersey City, and the same town recently renamed a portion of one of its streets after Dr. Babasaheb Ambedkar, the principal leader of the oppressed Dalit community[1] and chief framer of the Indian

1. Formerly called "untouchables", the Dalit are an Indian people who face severe discrimination by other Indians.

Constitution. Statues of Gandhi are to be found in numerous American cities, including New York City and Atlanta, and the US Congress has recently approved the construction, for which the expenses will be borne entirely by the Indian government and the Asian Indian community, of a memorial to Gandhi in the diplomatic enclave of the capital city, not far from the hallowed grounds where are to be found the memorials to Lincoln, Roosevelt, and Washington.

The Influence of Indian Politics on Indian Americans

What is most striking, however, is the manner in which the internal politics of India, and of the Indian subcontinent, is echoed in the politics of South Asian communities in the United States. When a portion of Chicago's Devon Avenue was renamed after Gandhi, the Pakistani businesses successfully applied pressure to have an adjoining section named after Jinnah, the founder of Pakistan. Much more dramatic, and rife with consequences, is the support rendered to various political movements in India among their adherents in the United States. As is now well-documented, the Sikh [a non-Hindu Indian people] separatist movement in the Punjab [a state of northwestern India] has received much institutional and financial support from Sikh militants in the United States, and the demand for an autonomous homeland, called Khalistan, continues to flourish among certain Sikh communities in this country even while it has become greatly attenuated in India. There are reliable reports of political violence within Sikh communities and even at gurudwaras [Sikh places of worship], where moderate Sikhs, as in India, have been targeted by their more militant and orthodox brethren. Such violent differences can assume other forms, as demonstrated by the dispute in Northern California over whether the kirpan, a dagger-like object that is an indispensable icon of the Sikh faith, can be taken to school by children. It is entirely pertinent that this issue only arose after the advent of the separatist movement, and was always clearly intended to deliver a message of faith to dissenting or apolitical Sikhs.

While Indian Muslims in the United States, whose numbers are in any case relatively small, have not been similarly vocal in stating their views on the insurrection now taking place in Kashmir [a politically divided region controlled by India, Pakistan, and China] the same can scarcely be said for those Hindus who continue to give their unstinting support to Hindu militancy in India. They rejoiced in the destruction on 6 December 1992 by Hindu militants of a sixteenth-century mosque, and have poured much money into the construction of a grand new Hindu temple in Ayodhya; and they contribute generously to the activities of the Vishwa Hindu Parishad (VHP), a world-wide organization set up to promote Hindu culture. . . .

Indian Contributions to Various Groups

As one considers the gamut of Indian political activity in the United States, there is reason to be hopeful as well. Some Asian Indians have undoubtedly contributed to the various movements which vigorously affirm the rights of cultural, religious, and ethnic minorities, that have energized the American landscape. The National Gay and Lesbian Task Force was for some years led by an Asian Indian woman, Urvashi Vaid, and prominent Asian Indian academics like Gayatri Spivak, who teaches at Columbia University, have forcibly lent their voices not only to the feminist agenda but to critiques of American global hegemony. There is room, as well, for progressive periodicals such as *SAMAR*, the South Asian Magazine for Action and Reflection, and *Trikone*, which is the organ of the Asian Indian gay and lesbian community. At the institutional level, while organizations such as the Network of Indian Professionals (NETIP) have, at least until recently, disavowed any significant interest in political questions, there are also explicitly politically minded organizations such as the Forum of Indian Leftists (FOIL) and the Committee on South Asian Women (COSAW), as well as organizations where second-generation Asian Indians with an eye to the American (rather than Indian) landscape often dominate, notably the India Abroad Center for Political Awareness and the Indian American Political Awareness Committee (IAPAC). If these organizations have rarely impacted American politics, it may also have to do with the fact that their membership is drawn largely from the academic world. . . .

A Lack of Political Enthusiasm?

It was for long a truism that Asian Indians were seldom involved in the political life of the nation, and for some years they have remained the only ethnic minority group that, as a whole, supports the Republican party. Nor does it augur well for their political awareness that, as Non-Resident Indians (NRIs), they appear to be more agitated and consumed by developments in India than they do by politics in the United States, however long their period of residence in the country that gives them their living. In recent years, there have been a number of Asian Indians who have unsuccessfully stood for election to Congress, and they show some signs of wanting to have greater involvement in American public life. But one hopes that Asian Indians will not confine their political activities to fund-raising for indistinguishable Democrats and Republicans, or accept the illusory mantra that elections equal democracy. The "glass ceiling" that has prevented the ascent of all Asian Americans to the highest political, managerial, and executive positions may have dimmed their political enthusiasm, but its real presence must not be allowed to obfuscate the recognition that Asian Indians have not shown themselves overly inclined towards political action and reflection. In this respect they might be partaking in the more general apolitical climate of the United States.

East Indians and the Impact of the September 11 Terrorist Attacks

Lavina Melwani

Many East Indian immigrants to the United States have achieved prosperity in their adopted land. East Indians are doctors, scientists, college students, independent business owners, and franchise operators and are highly visible in many American communities. In cities such as New York they are also taxi drivers, newsstand agents, and gas station attendants. The visibility of these working-class East Indians has sometimes led to their being singled out by racists who object to immigrants in general and to East Indians in particular. During the aftermath of the terrorist attacks of September 11, 2001, some East Indians (particularly Sikhs who wear turbans and beards) were mistaken for Arabs and were targeted for acts of retribution that ranged from vandalism to physical assault.

The following article by writer Lavina Melwani discusses the variety of hate crimes against East Indians. As she points out, East Indians of all economic backgrounds have become more willing since 9/11 to speak out against the violent acts of bigots or the government's activities that they believe threaten their personal and civil rights. They have formed new advocacy and human rights groups to speak out on their behalf.

Melwani is an East Indian American who writes regularly for Little India *magazine.*

"Unfortunately. . . he died a few minutes ago. (4:55 pm)." Just six words, but what a world of tragedy they enfold. Nabeel Siddiqui, 24, a computer science major who graduated

Lavina Melwani, "Hate Crimes Against Indians," *Little India*, http://littleindia.com, November 2003. Reproduced by permission.

from New Jersey Institute of Technology this summer [2003], suffered brutal neurological injuries and trauma when three juveniles attacked him with a baseball bat on his head at Haxtun Avenue in Orange, NJ, as he got out of his car to deliver a pizza. The three, a 16-year-old from Woodbridge and a 16-year-old and 17-year-old from Orange, have been charged with aggravated assault, robbery, carjacking, and possession of a weapon. Baseball and pizza. Such quintessentially all-American, joyful symbols. Yet why is it that a baseball bat, which one associates with sportsmanship, Little League innocence and camaraderie, turns into a killing machine when bigots see skin of a different hue? Pizza, that ubiquitous fast food, turns deadly when the deliveryman has an accent or comes from another culture. . . .

"The death of this young man is very symbolic of the violence that immigrant workers face in this country," says Bhairavi Desai, director of the New York Taxi Workers Alliance. She cites a survey of 581 drivers in which 24 percent experienced some kind of vandalism of their vehicle, 15 percent were physically threatened, 9 percent were physically harmed and 34 percent were verbally harassed. She adds, "These are extremely high numbers out of just 581 drivers; so imagine the number of incidents given that there are 24,000 active drivers in the industry." . . .

NAPALC [National Asian Pacific American Legal Consortium] reported that a large number of hate crimes in the aftermath of Sept. 11, targeted South Asian Americans, and more particularly Sikh Americans, because many wear turbans and beards, similar to the widely publicized image of [terrorist leader] Osama Bin Laden. According to the FBI, there were 36 victims of anti-Islamic bias in 2000. In 2001, the FBI figure jumped to 554 victims. According to NAPALC, the real figures could be very much higher than the FBI figures because law enforcement agencies do not classify a crime or incident as bias-motivated when there's only an account from a victim, the perpetrator has not been caught or there are no witnesses. The report cites language barriers, fear of police, fear of retaliation and fear of the INS [Immigration and Naturalization Service] as other causes of under-reporting hate crimes. Despite the Hate Crime Statistics Act of 1990, not all hate crimes are counted and documented. . . .

Who Faces Attack?

"How do you quantify human rights?" asks Desai. "The right to be safe in your society is a matter of a human right. It's really working class South Asians who get attacked. I know there's talk about jealousy of the Indians who are upwardly mobile, but it's the downwardly mobile Indians who face the attacks."

She points out that taxi drivers are 60 times more likely to be killed on the job than any other worker, according to the department of labor, followed by store clerks. Gas attendants, construction workers, and delivery persons—these are all professions dominated by black and brown immigrants, who often don't have the luxury of choice, when it comes to choosing a livelihood: "They are perceived to lack political power so they are seen as more vulnerable." . . .

The problem of hate crimes is not limited to blue collar professions. Racists do not differentiate between rich and poor immigrants; they are driven—like raging bulls—solely by color. Deepa Iyer, a co-founder of SAALT [South Asian American Leaders of Tomorrow], who was earlier a civil rights attorney with the Department of Justice in Washington, says, "I think it's a lot of anti-immigrant sentiment, where people say 'Go back to your country, you don't belong in our neighborhood.' So a lot of it has to do with a perception of who's American, who belongs in this country."

And as anyone living in America today or even flipping through an American newspaper knows, the situation has deteriorated markedly since 9/11 when the World Trade Center

attacks created so many new enemies, some real, some perceived. You could be born and brought up in America, may
have pledged allegiance to the flag since you were old enough
to recite the words, but if you are of a certain color or if your
features look remotely Middle Eastern, then all bets are off.
You could be Sikh, Hindu or Muslim, but suddenly you are
Osama, you are a terrorist and don't you dare deny it. . . .

The Impact of 9/11 on South Asians and Others

A survey of Muslims, Arabs and South Asians in New York . . .
released by the New York City Commission on Human Rights
found that 69 percent of respondents reported perceived discrimination and bias-related harassment. Almost one-third of
incidents involved religious and ethnic insults or physical as-
saults. Almost a quarter of the respondents reported employment discrimination, alleging that they had been taunted as
"Bin Laden" "terrorist" or "Taliban" in the workplace. According to the report very few reported the discrimination, the
majority because they felt either that nothing would be done,
or because they were afraid or uncomfortable reporting the
incident.

The report found that almost 4 in 5 respondents reported
that the events of 9/11 had adversely affected their lives, not-
ing: "A large number of individuals noted that they had al-
tered their behavior or manner of dress so as not to attract
notice. For example, they would speak only English in public,
cut their hair, shave their beards, wear hats instead of the hi-
jab [Muslim head covering], or Americanize their names.
Many said they were afraid to be in public places, and some
said they no longer go out as much or only go out with friends
and relatives. . . . Many spoke of being scared, stared at, in-
timidated, fearful, alienated, depressed, uncomfortable, cau-
tious, hurt, uneasy, ridiculed, shamed, misunderstood, sad,
blamed, insecure, scrutinized and emotionally stress[ed]."

As these bashings occur, one realizes that there are many baseball bats—literal and symbolic. Violence pervades our lives and as Desai points out, it includes physical attacks, verbal abuse, political disenfranchisement and economic impoverishment. We are living in violent times, an age of preemptive strikes and a seemingly endless war against terror. . . .

Indeed, sometimes it is hard to separate the bias crimes of ignorant bigots and those propagated by governmental policy, such as the mass detentions, raids at work, racial profiling and deportations that have plagued the Muslim community. Says Desai, "People in authority set the standard. The myth is that wealth trickles down, but the reality is that violence trickles down." The NAPALC audit points out the harsh facts of post 9/11 America, as the [George W.] Bush Administration targeted Arab and Muslim Americans in the name of homeland security. For example, it notes that the U.S. Department of Justice rounded up and imprisoned over 1,000 individuals of Arab and Muslim backgrounds without charge or allowing them access to attorneys.

The Department of Justice also publicly demanded that local police help them pressure 5000 Arab and Muslim immigrants to submit to interrogations and asked universities to turn over confidential files of students with Arab names. . . .

New Organizations for South Asians

The good news is that scores of organizations have arisen to meet the need, and victims can find support. As Iyer observes "Unfortunate as it was, 9/11 has provided an opportunity for the South Asian community to become a little bit more vocal and visible when it comes to furthering civil rights and human right[s] issues. I don't think we've got to the point where there is a 'South Asian-American' consciousness in our community but I think we're getting there slowly." There are now many more organizations for victims to turn to . . . , organizations where their language is spoken, their point of view embraced. Victims are encouraged not to take bias lying down. Recently Hansdip S. Bindra, a Sikh, filed a landmark lawsuit against Delta Airlines for racial profiling and harassment. He was aided by SMART [Sikh Mediawatch and Resource Task Force], founded in 1996, the oldest national Sikh American civil rights organization.

While many of the advocacy groups are composed of second generation Asians or South Asians, others are a collaboration between second and first generation groups. "Hate crimes are an issue which affects pretty much everybody and one is not insulated from these sorts of incidents just because of one's economic status or where one lives," says Iyer.

"Although poorer immigrants seem to get the brunt of it, it affects people from across economic lines and class lines because all of us have come from somewhere, all South Asians will feel some identification with 'Go back where you came from!' So it's an argument for people of all economic backgrounds to work together on this issue."

Young East Indians Defy Pressures to Conform to Parental Values

John Blake

In this selection journalist John Blake describes the dilemma faced by American-born East Indian young people who feel pressure from their tradition-minded parents to meet their expectations, including agreeing to arranged marriages, pursuing careers as engineers, doctors, or scientists, and becoming overachievers. Blake interviews four young East Indian Americans who describe how they have rejected some of their parents' plans to make their own decisions. Although disagreeing with their parents was difficult and stressful, the interviewees state that they had to be true to what they believe is right for their own lives.

Blake often writes about civil rights for the Atlanta Journal-Constitution *newspaper. He is also the author of* Children of the Movement, *profiles of the children of America's famous civil rights leaders.*

Four outlaws gathered at a Decatur [Georgia] coffeehouse to talk over their crimes.

One had married an African-American man. Another chose the wrong career. One is openly gay. The fourth, well, she just isn't submissive enough.

The group looked like a caramel-covered version of the cast of "Friends": four attractive, well-educated Indian-Americans brimming with confidence and laughter. But each has become an outlaw of sorts in Atlanta's South Asian community—people from India, Pakistan, Sri Lanka, Bangladesh and Nepal—because they've broken the rules for being a good South Asian, sometimes considered a "model minority" in America.

"You're supposed to be an engineer, a doctor, a scientist—anything that would make good money," says Sunita Patel, 22, of Decatur, who met with her friends at the coffeehouse on a recent evening.

The group then ticks off the rules: make straight A's, cheerfully agree to an arranged marriage, have fair skin or straight hair, and be submissive in public. And, whatever you do, don't act like African-Americans. "What's set up for you isn't realistic," says Deepali Gokhale, 30, a database consultant. "It's almost impossible to achieve the things you're supposed to achieve."

More than 70,000 South Asians now live in the Atlanta metro area, with the Indian-American population alone having recorded a 230 percent increase in Georgia from 1990 to 2000. Indians are also estimated to own nearly half the roadside hotels and motels in the state.

None of those numbers reflects the escalating divisions within the South Asian community, many of whose younger members say they're tired of being viewed as the "good minority": hardworking, submissive overachievers. They say this image has become an ethnic straitjacket that stifles individuality—and is often used to demean African-Americans by comparison.

Now they don't want to be examples anymore. They just want to be themselves.

Striving to Be Oneself

"You already have expectations set for you, so you can't set your own goals," says Agnes Scott College freshman Qudsia Raja, 18, a Pakistani-American.

Though she attends an elite school and plans on eventually working in international affairs, Raja says that wasn't good enough for her parents. She disappointed them, she says, by deciding not to become a doctor or agree to an arranged marriage. "Everyone talks about you," she says. "Everyone in the community knows who you are. It's a horrible feeling to know that I have all these expectations set before me and I can't keep up with them."

Most South Asians, however, eventually find a way to meet those expectations. They're consistently held up as a kind of gold standard among America's ethnic groups. The latest census figures indicate why: Divorce is low. At least 80 percent of South Asian households are maintained by married couples. The education level is high. More than 40 percent of South Asians age 25 or older have at least a bachelor's degree. Poverty is low. The group's poverty rate is only 10.7 percent.

Of course, the phenomenon of young adults feeling constrained by their parents' expectations is hardly unique to South Asians. In fact, Qudsia Raja's father, Tariq Raja, sounds like a lot of dads—a little surprised at her assessment. He says he's not disappointed that his daughter attends Agnes Scott and that he came to America precisely so she could have a good education and career options. "I give her my opinion, but I don't impose on her," he says.

The "Model Minority" Myth

But South Asians are a special case among ethnic communities in America. The "model minority" image is a myth built on a quirk of history, says Indian-born Vijay Prashad, author of *The Karma of Brown Folk*. Prashad, a professor at Trinity College in Hartford, Conn., says South Asians are disproportionately successful in America not because they are inherently more intelligent or work harder, but mostly because of immigration law.

In 1965, Congress passed the Immigration and Naturalization Act. The act was intended in part to fill the country's need for more scientists at the height of the space race with the Soviets, Prashad says. Most of the South Asians who subsequently immigrated to the United States fit the bill: They were the elite.

Between 1966 and 1977, Prashad says, 83 percent of Indians who immigrated to America entered under the category of professional and technical workers: about 20,000 scientists with Ph.D.s, 40,000 engineers and 25,000 medical doctors. Not surprisingly, those immigrants did well. Now, Prashad says, they expect their American-born children to follow the path they chose, right down to being top achievers at every level. "Parents are setting up INS [Immigration and Naturalization Service] standards for their kids," he says.

High expectations, most would agree, are more desirable than the low expectations and demeaning stereotypes that some other minority groups contend with. But Prashad notes that high standards can be very confining. "It's not human. It's like taking a group of scientists and making a colony on Mars and pretending the whole world should be scientists. Where are the artists, the poets, the drunks? Where is everybody that makes history possible?"

The high standards are reinforced by relentless parental and community pressure to conform. South Asian young people who don't conform to the myth, Prashad says, deny their parents access to the power centers of the community: joining the chamber of commerce, becoming a leader in the temple or heading a community organization. "The pressure on the child is enormous, and the parents suffer the embarrassment of their children not being the performing animals of their community."

Sunaina Jain, a family and child psychologist in Tucker, [Georgia,] says South Asian young people often feel torn between the outside world and the world inside their home. "They're living in a culture that's so individual, perhaps over-focused on individuality: what I want, what I feel, what my dreams are," she says. "South Asian culture is totally not about that. It's about we, the family, fitting in and living up to what's expected rather than having your own voice."

Conflict Between Generations

Jain, a native of India who has two daughters born in America, says many South Asian parents are terrified of their children becoming too American. "They see this as a permissive, wide-open society," she says. "I remember Indian parents who would send their daughters back to India when they reached 14 so they wouldn't date."

Raja shocked her parents when she told them she would not enter into an arranged marriage. Her habit of voicing her opinion in the presence of men also causes her mother anxiety. "She thinks I'll have problems later on when I get married," Raja says.

Sometimes the expectations can tear parents and children apart.

Sharmily Roy, 20, a junior at Agnes Scott, says she moved out of her parents' house two years ago because she did not fulfill their expectations. They wanted her to get an engineering degree at Georgia Tech. She chose Agnes Scott instead. "I have basically broken with them because I can't do what they want me to do," Roy says.

Career choice isn't the only land mine within the community. Marrying outside the ethnic circle and being homosexual both clearly fall outside acceptable behavior.

Aditya Kar, a native of India who now lives in Atlanta, is gay. When he returned home to tell his father this, he literally didn't have the words to break the news. "I was talking in Bengali to my father when I had to use the word 'gay,' but there's no equivalent word in Bengali to get the full meaning," he says. "I had to use the three exact in English: 'I am gay.'"

Kar, 36, says he once contemplated suicide because he thought something was wrong with him. His story was featured in a documentary about gay South Asians, "For Straights

Only," by Atlanta filmmaker Vismita Gupta-Smith. "If I had seen one South Asian face in my childhood or teenage [years] who said, 'I'm South Asian and I'm gay and it's OK,' I would not have thought of ending my life and probably used it in a more positive way," Kar says.

Sangita Chari fell headfirst into the tension between South Asians and African-Americans when she fell in love with a black man.

Racism in the Indian Community

Every South Asian interviewed for this article acknowledged that there is widespread racism within their community, with many routinely dismissing African-Americans as inherently lazy or prone to criminal behavior.

"If you're new to this country and you're watching television and you see one type of individuals who are committing crimes, that's what's going to come in your mind," says Aparna Bhattacharyya, director of Raksha, a nonprofit service organization for South Asians in metro Atlanta.

Chari, 30, met her husband in college. When they grew closer after dating for six months, she fretted over the prospect of marriage. Good Indian girls didn't marry black men. "It was a huge struggle for me," Chari says. "I felt like I was making a decision that would take me away from the Indian community."

"South Asians are status-conscious," says Jain, the psychologist. "If a man's daughter marries an African-American man, she's going to be subjected to all the prejudice already present in this society. She's going to be doubly different. Who wants that for his child?"

Chari says that, before she got married, she once decided to break up but couldn't find a good reason to do so. "I asked myself, 'If I give in and don't marry him just because he's black, then who am I?'" she says today.

Hidden Problems

Bhattacharyya says that dispelling the "model minority" myth would help the South Asian community. The community faces such problems as domestic violence, teenage suicide, homophobia and culture shock, she says, but they are rarely talked about openly because no one wants to dispel the myth. As a result, she says, the community can't get the help it sometimes needs.

Once, when Bhattacharyya applied for a foundation grant to help South Asian youths, she was told that she didn't need it because South Asian youths don't have problems. "I was so angry. We're always seen as the doctors and lawyers. People don't think we have people who are victimized."

Prashad wants South Asians to commit "model minority suicide" by being outspoken and individualistic and not allowing their success to be used to downgrade other people of color. "Why do I want a myth of success for myself when it's premised on the failure of others?" he says.

Chari, one of those who gathered at the coffeehouse, says she no longer lets others shape her identity. She says the decision has freed her. When others make the same decision, she says, it will liberate the South Asian community. "I'm Indian regardless of who I marry. I'm an American regardless of what anybody defines me as. If I buy into the myth, I'm not allowed to be so much of what I am. And we as a community are now allowed to be so much of what we are."

East Indian Youth Culture in New York City

Sunaina Marr Maira

Like all children of immigrants, young East Indians born and brought up in the United States fashion identities that combine elements of their home culture with elements of the larger multi-ethnic, multiracial society in which they live. In the following ex-cerpt from her book Desis in the House, *author Sunaina Marr Maira examines the youth culture of the desi club scene she ob-served in New York City. Desi (pronounced "they-see") is a San-skrit word meaning "of the motherland" and is used by South Asians living outside South Asia to refer to anything or any per-son related to their countries or culture. Maira describes the way desi youth mix classical dance moves of India handed down to them by their parents with Hindu film music, bhangra (a lively folk music and dance from the Punjab region of India), reggae, techno, and hip-hop. In Maira's view, the youth who take part in the desi club scene celebrate Indian culture through their use of traditional elements, but they also change the culture in subtle, unique ways. In clubs, for example, young East Indian women can wear low-slung, hip-hugging jeans their parents would al-most certainly disapprove of but sport traditional Indian nose rings. Their dance partners could be other East Indian youths as well as African American and white clubgoers.*

Maira is an assistant professor of Asian American studies at the University of Massachusetts in Amherst. She also coedited Contours of the Heart: South Asians Map North America.

The massive beats of a new sound reverberated in New York City nightlife in the mid-1990s, a mix of Hindi film music and bhangra, a North Indian and Pakistani dance and

Sunaina Marr Maira, *Desis in the House: East Indian Youth Culture in New York City.* Philadelphia: Temple University Press, 2002, pp. 29–34. © Temple University. All rights reserved. Used by permission of Temple University Press.

music, with American rap, techno, jungle, and reggae. The second-generation Indian American youth subculture that introduced this "remix music" has become a recognized part of the city's broader popular culture, heralded to the mainstream by concerts at the Summerstage series in Central Park, articles in the local news media, and documentaries by local independent filmmakers. . . .

Bhangra remix music constitutes a transnational popular culture in the Indian/South Asian diaspora; it emerged among British-born South Asian youth in the mid-1980s and has since flowed between New York, Delhi, Bombay, Toronto, Port-of-Spain [the capital city of the Caribbean nation of Trinidad], and other nodes of the South Asian diaspora. While this "remix youth culture" has emerged in other urban areas in the United States that have large Indian American populations, such as Chicago and the [San Francisco] Bay Area, its expressions are shaped by local contexts. There has not as yet been much comparative work on this topic, but it is clear that Manhattan lends this youth culture distinctive features, including particular sonic elements: DJ Tony of TS Soundz in Chicago pointed out to me that while Chicago remixes tend to use house and techno music, New York deejays favor remixes with rap music, and participants in this local subculture tend to adopt a more overfly "hoody," hip-hop-inspired style.

Desi Parties

The New York subculture based on Indian music remixes includes participants whose families originated in other countries of the [Indian] subcontinent, such as Bangladesh and Pakistan, yet insiders often code events that feature this music as the "Indian party scene" or "desi scene." While participants in the desi scene share certain South Asian cultural codes and common experiences in the United States, aspects of ethnic and national identity play out in particular ways for different national and religious, not to mention regional, groups. The "scene" is a differentiated one: Indian American youth who are not in college also attend these parties, and there are "Indian parties" held outside Manhattan, for instance, on campuses in New Jersey and Long Island that have large South Asian student populations. Manhattan, however, provides a particular context for desi parties because of the presence of city clubs, such as the Madison, the China Club, or S.O.B.'s (Sounds of Brazil), that draw large droves of South Asian American youth who get down to the beats of bhangra. S.O.B.'s, a world music club in downtown Manhattan, has been home to one of the most well known regular "bhangra parties" since March 1997, when DJ Rekha launched "Basement Bhangra," the first Indian remix music night to be featured monthly on the calendar of a Manhattan club—and the first to be hosted by a woman deejay. . . .

The music is remixed, or at least selected, by deejays who perform at parties hosted at local clubs, restaurants, and college campuses by promoters, generally young Indian American men and women, some of whom are college students who do this as a source of part-time income and who have helped create an urban South Asian American youth subculture. Nearly all the deejays that I met or heard about were Indian American, a point that deserves further reflection and that hints at broader questions about social networks within the clubbing industry and the dominance, or at least greater visibility, of Indian Americans within a purportedly pan-ethnic subculture. Information about desi parties circulates in a web of information that, when the scene began to flourish in the mid-1990s, initially could be hard for "outsiders" to break into. As in other dance cultures, remix parties are advertised through word of mouth, mailing lists, Web sites (such as the national www.desiparty.com), and flyers distributed at events, stores, clubs, and other places youth visit on the subcultural circuit. Every weekend, remix parties in Manhattan attract desi youth from New York, New Jersey, Connecticut, and even

Pennsylvania, areas that have large concentrations of Indian and other South Asian immigrant families as well as South Asian American student populations. Cover charges are steep but not atypical for New York parties, ranging from ten to twenty dollars, yet the parties draw hordes of youth from a range of class backgrounds who are willing to fork out money for leisure activities. Partygoers are for the most part second-generation, although some first-generation South Asian youth are usually in the crowd as well, participating in the redefinition of desi cool, in its urban, New York/Northeast incarnation, through the creative use of elements of popular culture. . . .

Mixing Clothing Styles

In conjunction with the fusion of musical genres, this subculture displays the construction of a culturally hybrid style, such as wearing Indian-style nose rings and bindis [ornamental mark on the forehead between the eyebrows] with hip-hop clothing and performing ethnic identity through dance, as in the borrowing of folk dance gestures from bhangra while gyrating to club remixes. Indian American women sported bindis long before pop stars Madonna and Gwen Stefani did, but they now do so in the context of commodified ethno-chic; mehndi kits—"Indian body art"—and bindi packets—"body jewels"—have sprouted in clothing stores, pharmacies, street fairs, and fashion magazines in the years since I completed this research. The mainstreaming of Indo-chic in the late 1990s is a hotly debated issue, especially among young desi women. . . .

April 4, 1997. The crowd thickens on the dance floor at S.O.B.'s, the music and darkness effectively blocking out all awareness of the street life just outside on Varick Street, in a largely commercial area of Tribeca in downtown New York. The club's space is small, with a few tables and mock palm trees scattered around the edges of the compact dance floor, in front of a raised stage area where bands occasionally perform. DJ Rekha spins in a tiny loft area that hangs over the bar and watches the crowd below as the insistent beat of the dhol, the percussion base of bhangra music, pounds out over the techno and reggae tracks reverberating amid the tightly packed bodies. Shoulders shrug and arms flail in semblances of bhangra moves, here, far from the wheat fields of the Punjab, far from the Californian orchards where early Punjabi migrants first settled in the early twentieth century.

Tonight, most faces are various shades of South Asian, but a few African Americans and White folks are getting down on the dance floor too, for this is one of the few bhangra club nights that draws a noticeably racially mixed crowd. One of the past Basement Bhangra events featured a booth with mehndi, lacy designs in henna, traced on palms by a young White woman riding the emerging fascination with Indian "body art." This night features an appearance by a live dhol drummer "all the way from Lahore," his yellow turban and sequined kurta [tunic] presumably authenticating the South Asian elements of this musical fusion. Boota Sheikh has an astonished, if delighted, expression on his face, as if simultaneously bewildered and excited by his performance for a frenzied crowd of young South Asians: women in hip-huggers twisting their arms in movements learned partly from Hindi films and partly from other bhangra nights like this, perhaps in college or at other Indian remix parties. A turbaned Sikh man leaps onto the stage beside the sweating musician, spinning and bouncing with acrobatic, breakdance-like agility. Jumping back into the crowd, he is joined by another young Sikh man, and as the crowd parts in a rapt circle, the two dance around each other in exuberantly coordinated precision. Then three young women who have various degrees of classical dance training step up to the circle, their fluid body movements evoking various genres of Indian dance, "filmi" and folk, and challenging what has been up to now an exclusively male, Punjabi performance. The women's enthusiasm on the dance floor is no less vigorous. The party has most certainly begun.

Many East Indian Immigrants Are Returning to India

Robert Weisman

Thousands of East Indians in the United States are choosing to return to live in India. Returnees are usually high-tech workers such as computer programmers or engineers, whose skills are transferable across national borders. In the following article, journalist Robert Weisman describes some of the reasons East Indians are going back to their homeland. Some are returning to start businesses in a country with a growing market and abundant supply of low-wage but highly skilled workers. Another factor influencing East Indians to return home is the need to care for aging parents, Weisman reports. Finally, some workers feel the tech sector in India is now growing faster than it is in the United States, and they want to be part of the boom. Weisman notes that the U.S. technology industry fears a brain drain as successful East Indians leave the United States to start companies in India.

Weisman is a staff reporter for the Boston Globe *and writes regularly on business topics.*

An Indian-born software developer, Pavan Tadepalli, wanted to work in a high-tech hub with opportunity for career growth. So it was an easy decision when he was offered a permanent job in the Boston area, after a three-month assignment here ended this spring [2005].

Tadepalli turned it down, and chose to return to India. "There are more opportunities in India now," he said. "What I can do in Boston, I am confident I can do the same thing in Hyderabad."

The lure of a career in the United States, especially in technology, proved irresistible to India's best and brightest engineering graduates through the 1990s, and even as recently as a few years ago.

But with the maturing of the US technology industry, and the rapid expansion of India as a center for software programming and business process outsourcing, thousands of Indian engineers and managers, many of them US-educated and working on Route 128 [Boston's high-tech zone] or in California's Silicon Valley, are opting to go back to their homeland.

The trend is raising fear of a brain drain. Some business leaders are worried that the immigrant Indian entrepreneurs who helped fuel the US technology boom might now start companies in India, and take whole classes of jobs with them.

"It could deplete the stock of educational and scientific talent that we have here," said Alan Tonelson, a research fellow for the United States Business & Industry Council, a Washington trade group for small and mid-sized manufacturers.

Advantages of Being a Returnee

American-educated graduates from other countries, from Israel to Taiwan to Ireland, also have launched companies in the United States. But the Indian connection is unique because of the intense engineering focus there.

And returnees starting businesses in India, unlike those in smaller and richer countries, can tap into a large and growing domestic market, and into a pool of low-cost skilled workers.

For some Indians, the reasons for the exodus are personal. Returning expatriates may have aging parents, or they may want their children raised in the Indian culture. But with the explosive growth of India's economy, cities such as Bangalore or Hyderabad increasingly are seen as new magnets for ambitious technologists offering an intoxicating mix of hefty raises, multiple job postings, and rapid career advancement, no longer the norm in Cambridge [Massachusetts] or in San Jose, Calif.

Joga Ryali worked in Silicon Valley for 22 years until he got an offer this year to run the Hyderabad product development center for Computer Associates, the computer software giant. He started there in June [2005].

"From a professional point of view, I felt until recently that I had more challenging prospects in the US," Ryali said. "But that's no longer the case. Just in the last couple of years, three or four of my close friends made the move from Silicon Valley to India. This feels in many ways like Silicon Valley felt . . . during the boom time."

Tadepalli's employer, the Indian outsourcing firm Sierra Atlantic, sent him to Boston in January to handle the merger with Sceptre Database Consultants, a Westwood [Massachusetts] company that was acquired by Sierra. By April, he had trained Sceptre employees in new technologies, worked with US customers, and set up processes enabling him to manage projects from India. "We established good communications," Tadepalli said. "Now we can do it by phone or email."

Neither the US nor the Indian government keeps count of how many Indian employees have left the American workforce to return to India. *The Economic Times*, a business publication in India, estimated that 35,000 have returned to the largest Indian high-tech center, which is now in and around Bangalore.

That is still a small fraction of the approximately 2.4 million Indian residents of the United States, a number that includes Indian-born residents as well as US citizens of Indian heritage. Massachusetts is home to an estimated 65,000 Indians.

A Diverse Group

The reverse migrants are a diverse lot. They include those who have graduated from American schools and return to India for their first jobs, and those who retire in India after spending their work lives in the United States. Many do business in both countries but still live in the United States, while some commute between homes in both countries.

Returnees say that India's substantially lower average wages are more than offset by its dramatically lower cost of living. And with the proliferation of Western amenities, from air conditioning to consumer electronics to shopping malls, the returnees say they have found that the American lifestyle is now available in India, at least for professionals laboring in the gleaming high-tech office parks of Bangalore and Hyderabad.

The impact of the exodus on the US economy is just starting to be felt. When he ran Taral Networks of Lexington, a wireless software company, Vinit Nijhawan was surprised that "one of my competitors came out of nowhere from India." With the emergence of a new generation of US-trained Indian entrepreneurs, "you can't be complacent about this any more," Nijhawan said.

The Impact on American Companies

Some business people say the trend will help both countries, though skilled American workers will have to adapt to new roles.

"The US is still going to be the idea lab and the funding lab, but the experiments will take place in India," said Upendra Mishra of Waltham, [Massachusetts,] chairman of the US-India Chamber of Commerce and publisher of the *Indus Business Journal* and *India New England* newspapers. "Then they'll bring the technology back to the US."

Gururaj "Desh" Deshpande, a cofounder and chairman of Sycamore Networks, an optical networking company in Chelmsford, [Massachusetts,] said the Indian technology boomlet will boost productivity for US companies by making simple functions cheaper. "The real innovation and brainpower will stay here," Deshpande said. "You can't create MIT [Massachusetts Institute of Technology] and Stanford and Harvard [universities] anywhere else in the world."

Businesses that operate in both countries can sometimes benefit by accommodating employees who want to return to India. But there can be a downside: Once they have moved workers back to India, companies find it tougher to retain them in the competitive job market, said Marc Hebert, executive vice president of Sierra Atlantic, which operates in Fremont, Calif., and Hyderabad.

"This is something new," Hebert said. "Three years ago, these retention problems didn't exist."

CHAPTER 4

COMING TO AMERICA

Profiles of Some Famous East Indian Americans

Samina Ali

Samina Ali, interviewed by Shauna Singh Baldwin

Many of the most accomplished East Indian writers live outside their native land in countries including the United States, Canada, and Great Britain. Some have immigrated for political reasons or for educational and professional opportunities. Others, such as novelist Samina Ali, were brought to the United States as children with their immigrant parents. In the following interview of Ali by Shauna Singh Baldwin, Ali describes her upbringing in both the United States and her birthplace of Hyderabad, India. She states that traveling back and forth between the two countries left her confused about whether she was Indian or American. However, Ali emphasizes that her experiences as a Muslim woman have strongly influenced her writing and her view of the world. Her debut novel Madras on Rainy Days *tells a story similar to her own: Layla is a young, educated Muslim woman who lives in India and America and and returns to India, where she is forced into an arranged marriage. Ali also states that the terrorist attacks of September 11, 2001, and the governmental scrutiny of Muslims that followed have made her realize how important it is for her and other Muslim writers to continue expressing their point of view even if the larger American society is reluctant to read it.*

Baldwin writes for the South Asian Women's Network.

Shauna Singh Baldwin: Which country/countries do you belong to legally/spiritually?

Samina Ali: I am an American citizen, naturalized when I was about eight. I was born in Hyderabad, India and immigrated with my parents to the US when I was close to 6 months old. I grew up in both places; it was important to my

Samina Ali, interviewed by Shauna Singh Baldwin, "Every Act Is Political: Samina Ali," www.sawnet.org, 2004. Reproduced by permission of the author.

father that his family not forget our heritage, meaning our Indian culture and Urdu language and religion of Islam, so he sent my two brothers, mother and me back to India every year. In India, I went to a Catholic school and I learned Urdu and Arabic and Indian English, and while here, I studied French and English. I grew up very confused and never knew what was my home. When I was in India, I wanted to be in the U.S., when in the States, I wanted to be in India. It was in India that I felt American and in America that I felt Indian—how is that for split identity! I remember Western travelers used to tell me how "at home" they felt in India, that it was their "spiritual home", but my own confusion really prevented me from understanding what they meant. It wasn't until I went to Italy in 2003 and spent some time there that I got it. Italy did feel like home to me, strangely, I did feel connected to the history, the people, the place. Spiritual home to me, then, implies a place where one journeys and feels roots that are imperceptible, indefinable. That's how I felt in Italy (and I've traveled to many places and not felt that).

India is my birthplace and home, my heart, my core. My first book, *Madras on Rainy Days*, is entirely set in Hyderabad because I wanted to start at the roots and then branch out. Now I feel comfortable writing about America in my second novel. Strangely, after the publication of my novel, I also finally feel at home in both America and India. It's almost as though the two places were dueling inside me, each trying to express itself, each with a distinct identity, and only when I gave a full voice to one and am about to give a full voice to the other that both are satisfied. Writing has brought me home.

Writing from a Muslim Perspective

SSB: Do you believe a writer can ever be apolitical? Should we [be]?

SA: I think there are many writers out there who are apolitical, who write simply to tell a story or who write simply to get published. Writing for writing's sake. I was at the LA [Los Angeles] Book Festival in 2004 and had this same question asked of me. There were four other panelists with me and all of them insisted that they were simply telling a story, nothing more. Three of those other writers are white males. When I finally spoke up, I seemed to have started a huge debate! What I said there is what I still believe: some of us simply do not have a choice but to be political in our writing. For instance, I am a Muslim woman. For many years now, there have been many other people telling the story of Muslim women.

Today, when Muslim women are the hot topic, the voices speaking out for them are still not Muslim. I am aware of what is being [said] about Muslim women and, more importantly, who is saying it. As such, it's very important to me to give a voice to my own experience and to have that one experience be expansive enough to include a general human experience even as I am dispelling stereotypes.

When I was trying to sell my book, I had editors ask me forthrightly to change parts of it: set half in the U.S. and half in India; have the American lover, Nate, storm Layla's wedding and "save" her, like a literary Rambo figure; show how Muslim women are repressed in India, denied their freedoms, asexual, while showing how America affords them freedoms they never dreamed up. Again, a perpetuation of stereotypes—worse, it would have been coming from a Muslim woman!

The act of writing for me is political. But for me, as a Muslim woman in post-9/11 America, almost every act is political: the way I dress, speak, present myself, raise my child, write!

A Violent Attack

SSB: At 19, I read that you experienced an attack by Hindus in Hyderabad. Have you drawn on that incident in your writing, yet? Was it in any way responsible for your becoming a writer?

SA: I grew up half in India so I grew up with military curfews and riots. This is simply part of life there, unfortunately, the civil unrest that results from tremendous political ambitions. The incident you're speaking about happened after I had gotten in my arranged marriage to a man back in India when I was 19. I had been married to him for close to six months by then and living with his family in a neighborhood that was predominantly Hindu. It was election season, which is when these old wounds get stirred, and a Hindu man came to our home one night and told us that our house was targeted. He said a gang of Hindu men was coming that same evening. We thanked him for informing us, but then there was nothing to do. It was dark so we weren't safe in trying to run away.

Our neighbors suddenly seemed like strangers or, worse, enemies. We had no phone, and even if we did, no police to call. Usually the police are involved in these crimes—remember, these are political crimes that manifest as religious ones. My mother-in-law, a conservative Muslim woman who only liked me to dress in loose shalwar-kameezes told me to put on jeans under my clothes—to further deter rape. She and I stayed in my bedroom all night, locked inside the house and then the room, while the men of the house went to the roofs. It was the worst night of my life. I thought I was going to die—with strangers!

My parents and brothers had already returned to the States and I believed I would never see them again. Then it occurred to me: here I am, having fulfilled each of my parents' dreams for me: I was the dutiful daughter who was doing a business major at university, who had gotten into an arranged marriage against her will to a Muslim Indian man, who had spent all her life traveling between two countries and two languages, and all for this! In all my parents' efforts in trying to keep me protected and safe, they had landed me at death's doorstep. Worse, I had allowed it to happen because I believed I didn't have a choice. I had handed over my life to them. I resolved that night that if I did ever make it back to the U.S., I was going to begin my life, lead it the way I wanted, and not be confined to my parents' and culture's and religion's expectations of me.

And that is what I did. The gang never did make it to our house. As in the novel, they did stop and murder a Muslim couple before they got to our house, and somehow this deterred them or they used up too much time, who knows, but we were saved. I will never forget though that I was saved at the price of a fellow Muslim sister's life. She was raped and murdered. I've written this exactly in the novel. I gave her a voice. I gave my story a voice. [Jewish novelist] Elie Wiesel says that writing is a way of saying, "this happened to me, this is the way it was, a way of saying 'Amen.'" Well, this did happen to me and this is the way it was, and now I say Amen!

The Impact of September 11

SSB: In an article in [the Indian newsmagazine] Rediff you say: "In the post-9/11 environment, Muslims are overtly discriminated against, stereotyped, demonized. Muslim men are seen as terrorists and 'evil,' controlling and dominating women. Muslim women are seen as sexually repressed and uneducated, their bodies and movements controlled. I hope the novel exposes Western readers to ordinary Muslims and thereby humanizes them. I also hope Layla can prove that a woman, even a Muslim woman, can come out from under the weight of tremendous familial and cultural expectations to become her own person." Post 9/11/01, has there been any change in your editor/publisher's perception of your work? Did the attack on the World Trade Center affect the willingness of US editors to publish your work?

SA: Most people think that selling a book after 9/11 must have been easy for a Muslim woman. It really wasn't. I was writing about Muslims, yes, but certainly not writing about what others wanted to hear. In hindsight, it makes sense to me that FSG [Farrar, Straus & Giroux] published my book without changes to my message. The publishing house does a marvelous job of publishing writers from places like South Africa and other politically charged areas of the world, places that cannot be excused or lied about, and neither, unfortunately, can the story I've written. Not only did the publishing become more difficult, but the audience is also more reluctant to see the message. I'm working against many stereotypes and machines of power, and Muslims have no power right now. So any change I make will be slow yet valuable.

SSB: Did the attack on the World Trade Center on 9/11/01 and the threat of terrorism/being labelled a terrorist affect your writing life in any way?

SA: I've not written a new work since 9/11 so I'm not sure how it will affect my characters. However, I am working on a novel right now, just at the beginning of one, and I am working through this very issue. I'm not sure how to touch the topic because it is so loaded.

Interestingly, there are young American writers I know of out there who have already published on the subject, even moving their characters into Iraq and telling the story from the Iraqi point of view, but I cannot write something without fully digesting it in all its nuances. I wouldn't feel responsible as a writer or thinker or human. Since my characters are Muslim, it's especially important that I understand and present this accurately. The larger Muslim community in America has really been supportive of my work and my message, and the weight of their faith does give me courage to proceed.

Receiving Extra Scrutiny

SSB: Have you experienced racism or have you been targeted as a visible minority in your home town or while travelling? Has there been an increase since 9/11/01?

SA: Fortunately, I haven't, but I know it's because of the way I look and people's ignorance: no one knows how to place me; even other Indians sometimes ask me where I come from! I've traveled with my two brothers, however, and both are men who are over 6 feet tall with black hair and dark eyes, Muslim names and faces, and it's a hassle. They get stopped at least three times even before they reach the line for the security check. Then they get pulled over again.

A few times I've been stopped at the airport while trying to check in. I was told my name was on the "terrorist list" and it would take 45 minutes to clear up. God knows what they then do to "clear this up," but in those 45 minutes to an hour, I sit and fume! Yet it always comes down to this: we are all doing this to each other. Muslims and non-Muslims alike. There is no one to blame.

Ismail Merchant

Ismail Merchant

In 1958 twenty-two-year-old Ismail Merchant left his middle-class home in Bombay for the United States. He planned to study for a master's degree in business administration at New York University. Merchant's arrival in America began his odyssey into the world of filmmaking and a career producing more than forty films, including A Room with a View, Remains of the Day, *and* Howard's End. *The following excerpt is taken from Merchant's autobiography* My Passage from India. *As Merchant points outs, his idea of America was colored by the Hollywood films he saw as a boy. Yet his early days as a newcomer in the United States were hardly glamorous. He moved frequently, struggled to learn about New York and its customs, and looked for work. However, the stress of being an immigrant did not diminish Merchant's enthusiasm for America. Like many East Indian immigrants, Merchant appreciated America's youthfulness, informality, and sense of optimism. He describes his adopted home of New York City as a place of energy and opportunity. Eventually Merchant found a partner in American director James Ivory, and together they became one of the most enduring filmmaking teams in history. Merchant died in 2005 at the age of sixty-eight.*

In my fourth and final year at St. Xavier's [College in Bombay], I began to apply to American universities for admission to postgraduate business schools. I wrote to all the obvious places: Harvard, Yale, the University of Chicago, New York University and, of course, the University of Southern California, which was on the doorstep of Hollywood and, therefore, from my point of view, the ideal choice. New York University

Ismail Merchant, *My Passage from India: A Filmmaker's Journey from Bombay to Hollywood and Beyond*. New York: Viking Studio, 2002, pp. 22–7. Copyright © Ismail Merchant, 2002. Used by permission of Viking, a division of Penguin Group (USA) Inc.

was the only one that offered me a place, and I was thrilled to receive the acceptance. Even though New York was a long way from Hollywood and I had never been there, it was a city I felt I knew intimately. This knowledge came from the movies, especially the Rock Hudson and Doris Day comedies that painted New York with a glamour and sophistication that made it seem like my kind of town. Every New York street was, according to the movies, paved with gold.

There was only one drawback: I didn't have the funds to pay the university fees. My father's resources were limited, and he could only provide a portion of the costs. My fellow students at St. Xavier's with whom I had worked to put on the college shows over the years now took it on themselves to organize a variety show ... They raised twenty thousand rupees—a fortune in those days—and, touchingly, gave that money to me as a gift toward my American studies. During our time at college we had combined our individual talents in art, music and theater to form an adventurous and very successful group that contributed to one of the strongest and most influential periods of St. Xavier's history. Later, when I began making films, I found myself repeating this process, bringing together talented individuals whom I would work with again and again over the years.

Leaving Bombay

I left Bombay for New York on August 11, 1958, taking the boat from Bombay to Genoa, then the train to London, where I would spend a few days with my friend Karim before flying to New York.

Karim and I had grown up together virtually as brothers, our families being very close. He was a year ahead of me at St. Xavier's College, and was already a year into his law studies in London. He came to meet me at London's Victoria Station, where I felt a little chilly in spite of the August day. We took a taxi to his lodgings in Hampstead, and he introduced me to his landlady, a frosty, unwelcoming woman. "How," I asked Karim, "do you keep warm here?" Karim showed me a small gas fire, which also heated the water for a bath, that came to life only if you fed coins into a nearby slot meter. This seemed a very expensive way to keep warm and clean. Not that I really minded. I was in London. The London of [the movie] *Brief Encounter*, and early [Alfred] Hitchcock movies where the city always seemed to be shrouded in fog. It was also the London of history books and literature: Queen Victoria, Disraeli, Shakespeare, Wordsworth. Suddenly all the names I had grown up with had a context: Buckingham Palace, the Houses of Parliament, Big Ben and Westminster Bridge all lay before me, solid and inviting. . . .

There was a moment when I seriously considered staying in London: I liked the place; Karim was there, and through him I had met other people. The prospect of going to New York, where I would be on my own, suddenly seemed daunting. But, to coin a terrible cliché New York was calling me. I knew my destiny lay there.

Arrival in New York

Disillusion set in within hours of my arrival in New York. My home was a dingy room on the sixteenth floor of the Martinique Hotel in Herald Square, an area whose streets were not so much paved with gold as with inebriate bums clutching their bottles of cheap liquor. The chances of bumping into Doris Day or Rock Hudson as I walked around the neighborhood suddenly seemed very remote. And I was unlikely to encounter them in the local Horn & Hardart [automat], where I was introduced to the novel concept of coin-operated food. Everything seemed to work on the principle of the slot machine. I had been lured to New York by the make-believe world of the movies, and had been terribly let down. "What have I come to?" I asked myself "What kind of a place is this?"

Ismail Merchant. Getty Images

My dreams were shattered—so far removed was this experience from the celluloid promise.

The next day I took a taxi to the International House on Riverside Drive at 123rd Street, and as the driver negotiated the Upper East Side and Century Park, cutting through areas that seemed more inviting and interesting, things started looking up. The International House, which is run by the Rockefeller Foundation, was where a number of students who had traveled on the boat from Bombay were staying, and I thought I might be able to get a room there too. I put my name on the waiting list, and no sooner had I returned to the hotel than I got a call from International House telling me that a room had become temporarily available, so I packed my bags and bid good-bye to the Martinique.

I remember getting my first letter from home and then bursting into tears with homesickness. I felt like a gypsy, moving from one place to another, unsettled and still unfamiliar with my surroundings. And there was worse to come. When my time was up at International House, I found a room in an apartment on the Upper West Side. The landlady was German and so terrifying that I dreaded coming face-to-face with her, so I would peep through the keyhole of my room to make sure she wasn't around before sneaking into the kitchen or the bathroom. The other two lodgers, a construction worker and a disabled man in a wheelchair, were equally weird, and the whole scenario seemed to belong in a horror movie.

Meanwhile, because I had very little money, I had to find a job. I went to the Indian Consulate and finessed my way into the office of Mr. Ayer, the secretary of the Indian Mission, who needed some additional staff to take care of the delegates arriving from India to attend the annual General Assembly. "Do you know New York?" he asked. "Oh, yes," I replied. "I know New York very well." The job paid ninety dollars a week, part-time. There was no other answer I could have given.

I went down to Washington Square to enroll at New York University. I loved the park, the architecture of the brownstones, the cobbled streets and, above all, the young people who inhabited the area. I knew I could be happy there, and wanted to find a room or an apartment to share in that neighborhood. I was so desperate to move out of the German stalag that when another temporary vacancy became available at International House, I jumped at it. I was delighted to discover a close friend from St. Xavier's there and, together with a friend of his, we decided to rent an apartment in Brooklyn Heights.

One of the first things I did was to visit the Empire State Building. I took the tour to the very top of what was then the tallest building in the world, and half expected to see King Kong swinging from the pinnacle. I was standing on the top of the world and, as I looked across New York, I knew this was the place to be, this was the place where one could prove oneself. It is impossible to look down from the Empire State Building at the view of that great city, radiating opportunity and promise, and not be filled with a sense of energy and optimism. No matter how bleak my life seemed at that moment, I knew the movies hadn't lied. New York was the greatest city in the world, even if, at ground level, things didn't look quite so rosy. The message from the top of the Empire State Building was clear: This is New York and anything is possible.

Vijay Iyer

Vijay Iyer, interviewed by Manu Vimalassery

The son of Indian immigrant parents, Vijay Iyer was born and raised in upstate New York in the 1970s. He began violin lessons at the age of three and began picking out melodies on the piano at the age of six. A self-taught pianist, Iyer became interested in jazz in his teens and began performing original music in college. At the same time he earned a master's degree in physics followed by a PhD in music and cognitive science from the University of California at Berkeley. In recent years he has released many acclaimed recordings and has traveled around the world to perform at jazz concerts and festivals. In the following interview by Manu Vimalassery of SAMAR (South Asian Magazine for Action and Reflection), Iyer describes how he creates music and how his Indian heritage influences his compositions. He notes that his relationship to this heritage is complicated and that he has also been influenced by many aspects of American culture as well. In following his dreams, Iyer states, he hopes he can inspire other young East Indian Americans to pursue their own interests and widen their sense of what is possible.

Vijay Iyer, New York-based composer, pianist, improviser, and scholar, has been at the forefront of South Asian American culture and music emerging in the past decade. His body of work remains distinctive in its probing of the aesthetics of music performance and composition, simultaneously embracing and speaking through political positions, all while engaging current philosophical debates. His major recordings include *Memorophilia, Architextures, Panoptic Modes,* and *Blood Sutra* under his own name; *Your Life Flashes,* as the trio Fieldwork; and *In What Language?* in collaboration with poet/ performer/producer Mike Ladd. He has performed around the

Vijay Iyer, interviewed by Manu Vimalassery, "Hybrid and Alive," *SAMAR*, no. 17, 2004. Reproduced by permission.

world with his ensembles and collaborations, including the multimedia performance *In What Language?*, the Vijay Iyer Quartet, Fieldwork, and Raw Materials, his duo with saxophonist Rudresh Mahanthappa.

Iyer has also performed, toured, and recorded extensively with artists such as Steve Coleman, Roscoe Mitchell, Amiri Baraka, Dead Prez, Butch Morris, Miya Masaoka, Trichy Sankaran, Imani Uzuri, Will Power, and Burnt Sugar, among others. His recent album, *In What Language?* (Pi Recordings, 2003), was lauded as a powerful political and artistic statement in *Billboard* and *The Village Voice*. His latest quartet album, *Blood Sutra* (Artist House, 2003), was the highest-ranking independent release in the *Jazz Times* 2003 critics' poll. Iyer took some time out of his busy *schedule* to share some of his considerable knowledge and insight on aesthetics, politics, and identity with *SAMAR* 's Manu Vimalassery.

Iyer's Unique Musical Style

Manu Vimalassery: A lot of the highly visible music in the South Asian diaspora tends to use instruments or instrumental sounds associated with South Asian music. Your music tends not to use these instruments, although you use rhythmic and melodic forms from South Asian musical traditions, in communication with structures and forms from jazz, which has a very different ideal listener and concert form than the other South Asian diaspora music. Do you feel your music addresses a similar audience as these other styles?

Vijay Iyer: I've listened to and learned from a large range of music from around the world, and nowadays I tend to hear music as both ritualistic and discursive in nature. That is, music provides an occasion to bring people together and place a heightened, collective experience in their bodies, but it also carries messages to those people, and it produces its own meanings. And this is true of instrumental music as well; there is a real exchange of information taking place in music, which is not often discussed even though it's undeniable.

I think the main difference between the other instances you mention and my own music is that perhaps my music's emphasis is slightly more on the discursive side. That isn't to say that the ritual side is not operative as well in my work; I use a lot of cyclical rhythmic/groove-based concepts associated with ritual, along with much attention paid to sensation and emotion. I also don't mean to suggest that the discursive is not operative in dance-oriented forms like bhangra [a form of folk music and dance from India's Punjab region] or the Asian underground. Of course, these elements are always active to varying degrees. But my work is meant not just as a soundtrack to an environment, which is how a lot of listeners treat music these days; rather, it is meant primarily *as a form of address*.

Because of this, my ideal listener is someone who is willing to engage actively with music in this way, and for whom music functions not just to entertain, or to accompany a social occasion, but also to provoke thought, to unsettle, and to question. That doesn't mean that there is no overlap with the audiences for Panjabi MC; it's just that these listeners have to be open to a different kind of musical experience.

I say all this because I think it's more accurate than saying "this is jazz, and this is pop" or whatever. I take such categories with a grain of salt.

Exploring the Meaning of Music

Manu Vimalassery: How does the internal discourse of your music—especially in your instrumental music—interact with non-musical discourses? Especially in terms of titles, such as some of the songs from your album Blood Sutra, *like "Habeas Corpus". Do you feel that you have control over these discourses, or do you think they take shape in relationship with your audience?*

Vijay Iyer: I've been thinking about this a lot lately. "About-ness" in the case of instrumental music is never obvious. In the past I've made assertions that certain instrumental pieces were "about" some issue or another, for example, on my 2001 album *Panoptic Modes* I had a piece that was dedicated to Rishi Maharaj [an Indian-American who was the victim of a racial attack in 1998], and another that was dedicated to Mumia Abu-Jamal [a journalist and political activist who was convicted of the murder of a police officer in 1981], still another dedicated to the people of Iraq under sanctions. I made this clear in the disc's liner notes; in keeping with these concerns, the music displayed its share of rage, yearning, mournfulness, and ambiguity.

In my more recent instrumental album *Blood Sutra*, though the work is coming from the same critical politicized perspective, I was thinking more about how instrumental music works. Its strength is that it asks more questions than it answers; it sets up a field of possibilities, in the way that poetry does, and it also works on the sensations. These pieces all came from being in New York after [the terrorist attacks of] 9/11 and trying to make sense of it all, as we all were. So that music came from a dense emotional place of grief, rage, sympathy numbness, and disbelief. We were all trying to understand the history that brought us to where we are, responding to the atmosphere of panic, fear, and shameful intolerance that followed in this country, and ultimately trying to get back to the experience of love in spite of it all.

The music on that album is a series of pieces related in some way to the word "blood," in all of its associations: family, disease, race, ethnicity, violence, desire. But beyond that, I didn't see fit to clamp down any one piece to a single association or interpretation, beyond the titles and the suggestions that they carried with them. So I let go of the insistent "explanations" of what each piece was "about." It was maybe about something specific when I composed it, but in collaborative improvisatory performance, so much else happens. Really, if it's played with commitment and authenticity and grounded in the perspectives that we share, each piece is about everything, or nothing; it's about a certain time and place in our lives, and everything that happened to us. Because these pieces feature so much improvisation, they're really exploding with meaning. . . .

The Collaborative Process

Manu Vimalassery: In a way, it seems that your music speaks through a channel of identity, or speaking from a particular voice, but develops that voice in relationship to a series of others, where the end result blurs the lines, or explodes the possibilities of clear and coherent identities in the outcome. Is this a conscious strategy on your part? If so, how do you try to convey it musically?

Vijay Iyer: I put a lot of faith in the collaborative process, which is the space where this phenomenon emerges. I never stop "being myself" in a collaboration; I can only improvise and compose from my own knowledge and aesthetics (which are always in flux but are also pretty well-defined—I'm too opinionated to go along with stuff I don't like!). But I am also forced to highlight different aspects of myself in different collaborative contexts, and also to develop and grow beyond what I already know, to meet the other people somewhere in between. And this is true whether I'm working with other desis [people of South Asian descent], or with African Americans, or anyone else, young or old.

Something that we as desis [pronounced, "they-sees"] are always up against, which I try to address in my aesthetic and collaborative decisions, is the notion of mobility. If we are always seen as "ethnic" and "particular," then no one else ever has to imagine that they have any points of contact with us, outside of what they see as our quaint little sphere. We are rarely permitted to have any larger impact in the world.

We should work to confound all of that, by claiming our place in a larger conversation. This is where we have so much to learn from African American culture. I think of people like Jimi Hendrix, or Duke Ellington, or John and Alice Coltrane, or Paul Robeson, or Nina Simone—uncompromising artists and thinkers whose work had such a searing clarity that it harkened a new reality, something towards which we could all aspire.

In What Language?

Manu Vimalassery: We seem to be in the midst of a re-conceptualization of the coherency and usefulness of a South Asian American identity, especially in response to the War on Terrorism. This comes through, for example in [professor of business at Rider University] Biju Mathew's editorials on identity-based organizing in the two most recent issues of SAMAR, and in scholars and activists re-aligning South Asian Americans with Arab Americans, away from Asian Americans. Did you find it necessary to confront these issues when you were putting together In What Language?

Vijay Iyer: These issues were in fact the basis of the *In What Language?* project. When I heard about Iranian filmmaker Jafar Panahi's pre-9/11 INS ordeal at JFK,[1] I saw it as emblematic of an issue common to the entire "Brown Atlantic." It became clear that for me to develop a project that felt relevant and real, I had to address not just being South Asian but being brown and transnational in the West, in an age of increasing global panic and suspicion. Collaborating with poet/hip-hop artist Mike Ladd (librettist/performer/co-producer for *In What Language?*) made this idea even larger, because he's a mixed African-American who is often taken for Arab or Latino. Mike's opening lines describe "the delicate distance of

1. Panahi was arrested by Immigration and Naturalization Service officers at New York's John F. Kennedy Airport for not having a transit visa and for refusing to be finger-printed.

brown" and "the uneasy proximity of tan"—evoking this third-world mutability in relation to the international privilege we possess as Americans. . . . It's so important to maintain a historical perspective and understand our own struggles in relation to others, and to understand what realities shape our uneasy proximities. The airport is such a metaphorically rich site for the investigation of these issues, so we made that the setting for this song cycle.

Incidentally, we received some hate speech (or maybe hater speech would be more accurate) on the Amazon.com page for the *In What Language?* album. Someone criticized our focus on issues facing "people of color," saying that those issues don't compare to the enormity of the WTC [World Trade Center] attacks. He called it "whining in the face of real tragedy," as if to suggest that the attacks somehow invalidate any kind of oppositional critique or inquiry. It's sad but unsurprising.

The Complicated Role of Identity

Manu Vimalassery: What role do you think identity plays as a motivating force, as well as a burden of representation, in your music, especially in relationship to these same questions with the other styles of South Asian diaspora music?

Vijay Iyer: Perhaps for a lot of desis, the attitude toward those other forms you mention is something like: this is the music that my parents listened to, but now with a beat that I can dance to. Or this music creates a safe space where I can be fully desi with my desi friends, where we can participate in the same clubbing rituals that non-desis can indulge in everywhere else.

All of these attitudes are valid and important, but to me there's sometimes a danger of self-exoticization. Even in certain cases where the music is made "for us—by us," if we are in view of the mainstream, that dynamic is always in play. It can reach the point where that gesture of incorporation of difference into the mainstream—what [cultural studies expert] Stuart Hall identified as a hallmark of the "global postmodern"—is the primary function of such music. It lets us indulge our self-orientalizing fantasies, in which we suddenly become desirable or cool because we're desi; it lets the mainstream feel like they're being more tolerant, inclusive, "global."

In many cases people listen to the music and think: cool, that's electronic but it's also exotic; it's modern but it's also ancient; it fuses x (the familiar) and not-x (the unfamiliar). In this logic, we still get put in the not-x box, so nothing has really been undone.

Iyer's Childhood Influences

My own relationship to South Asian music is not very simple, so I would feel dishonest simply foregrounding South Asian sounds, and not acknowledging other sides of myself. I didn't grow up with tabla [an Indian percussion instrument] lessons or with Bollywood movies [lavishly made Indian films]; my parents are urban Tamils [people from southern India and Sri Lanka], and I grew up in a time and place (upstate NY in the 70s and 80s) where we didn't really have access to a lot of supposed hallmarks of Indian culture and my immigrant parents weren't all that attached to that stuff anyway. I grew up with occasional bhajans [songs for worship or offering prayers] and Michael Jackson, brief doses of Karnatak [a southern state in India] music and Hindu ritual, a lot of Beethoven, *Saturday Night Fever*, math club, rice & sambar [a south Indian dish] Pizza Hut, the Police, Star Wars, Prince, and (more than anything else) the experience of being dark-skinned with a "foreign" name in suburban America, trying to figure out how to *be*.

I have to imagine that this is what childhood was like for lots of other people in my generation; it wasn't just about being Indian, but being utterly hybrid, and brown, and mystified by it all. So in my own music, more than anything else, I just try to tap into that mystery of being hybrid and alive. I make music that tries to make sense of my world, not as a representative of a subcontinent, but as one individual among many in our diverse communities, sitting at the confluence of many different streams.

For me one of the most important aspects of this "identity" thing is the possibility of providing a template for others to identify with. When I travel around and perform, I am able to provide an example or a precedent for other young people from our community. It's happened many times, this act of connection with South Asian American (or other Asian American) students and youths, often just as they're trying to figure out how to *be in the world*. Typically they don't tend to have a broad notion of what their options are, but if they see me performing alongside a legendary figure like [African-American poet and writer] Amiri Baraka, or leading my own group, or in collaboration with [jazz saxophonist] Rudresh Mahanthappa, they might feel inspired to pursue their own dreams. So I'm glad to be able to suggest alternative possibilities, just by the sheer *fact* of doing what I do.

And the flipside of that is the possibility that someone from outside our communities might be able to identify with someone like me. This is a power of music and the arts, to create an occasion where people can suddenly recognize themselves in the work of someone "different" from them.

Sabeer Bhatia

Stuart Whitmore

Many young East Indian technologists took advantage of the interest in the Internet and Web-based industries to create innovations—and make personal fortunes in the process. Sabeer Bhatia is one of the most famous of these young entrepreneurs. He cofounded the Internet-based e-mail service Hotmail and sold it to Microsoft in 1996 for $400 million. According to journalist Stuart Whitmore, the author of the following selection, Bhatia was entrepreneurial from a young age and opened up a sandwich shop in his hometown of Bangalore (India's technological center) while still in high school. While his parents hoped he would take a job in a multinational corporation after university, Bhatia had other ideas. He gained a full scholarship to the California Institute of Technology and left India to make his fortune in America. While working for Apple Computers, Bhatia, with his cofounder Jack Smith, came up with the idea of creating a way to access e-mail from any computer, and Hotmail was born.

Bhatia typifies many of the qualities shared by other Indian American entrepreneurs. His parents valued education and encouraged him to study hard. Upon arriving in the United States alone and uncomfortable with the language and culture, Bhatia stuck it out. Hard work, determination, and focus brought him success, but only after many investors had rejected his business plan. Through it all, Bhatia has remained humble and at ease with his fame.

Whitmore is a journalist who writes on Asian business and business leaders.

When he was only 28, Sabeer Bhatia got the call every Silicon Valley entrepreneur dreams of: Bill Gates wants to buy your company. Summoned to Microsoft's command

Stuart Whitmore, "Driving Ambition," *AsiaWeek.com*, June 25, 1999. Reproduced by permission.

bunker in Redmond, Washington state, he was deposited on the new acquisitions conveyor belt. Round and round the Microsoft campus he went. All 26 buildings. At every stop, Bhatia's guide helpfully pointed out the vastness of the Microsoft empire. The procession ground on until it reached Gates's office. Bhatia was ushered in. Bill liked his firm. He hoped they could work together. He wished him well. Bhatia was ushered out. "Next thing is we're taken into a conference room where there are 12 Microsoft negotiators," Bhatia recalls. "Very intimidating." Microsoft's determined dozen put an offer on the table: $160 million. Take it or leave it. Bhatia played it cool. "I'll get back to you," he said.

Eighteen months later Sabeer Bhatia has taken his place among San Francisco's ultra-rich. He recently purchased a $2-million apartment in rarified Pacific Heights. The place looks like a banker's lair, and Bhatia acknowledges that the oak paneling and crystal chandeliers might have to go. He hurries over to picture windows that run the length of the room and raises the blinds. Ten floors below, the city slopes away in all directions. The Golden Gate Bridge, and beyond it the Pacific, lie on the horizon. "This is me," he says. "I bought it for the view."

His Vision

A place with a view for a man with a vision. A month after Bhatia walked away from the table, Microsoft ponied up $400 million for his startup. Today Hotmail, the ubiquitous Web-based e-mail service, boasts 50 million subscribers—one quarter of all internet users. Bhatia is worth $200 million. He is already working on his followup: a "one-click" e-commerce venture called Arzoo! And Bhatia is looking homeward with an ambitious plan to wire India.

Bhatia was born and raised in the southern Indian city of Bangalore. His father, [Balev,] who held a high post at the Ministry of Defense, and mother, Daman, a senior official at a state bank, placed great value on education. Their only son did not disappoint them. "On parent-teacher days they would just say 'Sir, why did you come? You don't have to come! We tell Sabeer to solve the questions on the blackboard for us,'" says Bhatia senior. Once Sabeer came home crying after an exam. He had not done badly; he just hadn't had time to write down everything he knew.

Like many Indian parents, Balev and Daman hoped their son would secure a lifetime position with a big multinational firm. Sabeer had different ideas. "I was pretty entrepreneurial even as a schoolboy," he says. When a college opened nearby, he decided to open a sandwich shop and drew up his first business plan. "Then my mom said 'Stop thinking about these things and go and study.' But that's the culture in India."

Maybe mother knew best. In 1988, Bhatia won a full scholarship to the California Institute of Technology, in Pasadena. When his plane touched down that fall, 19-year-old Bhatia had $250 in his wallet and butterflies in his stomach. "I felt I had made a big mistake," he says. "I knew nobody, people looked different, it was hard for them to understand my accent and me to understand theirs. I felt pretty lonely." Ten years later you can still catch a glimpse of the innocent abroad. The Westcoast accent retains the sing-song cadence of his native Hindi. The CD collection features Bollywood [Indian movie] soundtracks and dance remixes of traditional Indian tunes. Yet Bhatia wears his American-style success easily, comfortable with his wealth yet unconsumed by it. His confidence and boyish modesty is an attractive blend that lends Bhatia serenity and presence, sending friends and associates into rapture.

Persistence and Focus

People say when Bhatia enters a room he owns it. "I call him the Hindu Robot," says Naveen Singha, Bhatia's friend, mentor and proud owner of the third-ever Hotmail address. "He is persistent, focused, disciplined. He's a superior human being." Others say he glows with a beatific, otherworldly air. On our way to his office, Bhatia attempts a U-turn in his midnight-blue Porsche Boxster, stalling the slick little roadster across two lanes of traffic—and in the path of a garbage truck. "I'm not superhuman," Bhatia says. Rather, he has joined the ranks of the over-hyped Silicon Valley celebrities he idolized. Doing his masters of science at Stanford, Bhatia attended lectures by such legends as Steve Jobs of Apple and Scott McNealy and Vinod Khosia of Sun Microsystems. Listening to them speak, Bhatia "realized they were human. And if they could do it, I could do it too."

After Stanford, Bhatia found work as a hardware engineer at Apple. "I think my parents expected me to stay for 20 years," he says. Bhatia lasted nine months. In his cubicle, he read about young men starting up for peanuts and selling out for millions. Bhatia pondered what the Net could do for him, and what he could do for the Net. Then he had an idea.

It was called Javasoft—a way of using the Web to create a personal database where surfers could keep schedules, to-do lists, family photos and so on. Bhatia showed the plan to Jack Smith, an Apple colleague and they got started. One evening Smith called Bhatia with an intriguing notion. Why not add e-mail to Javasoft? It was a small leap with revolutionary consequences: access to e-mail from any computer, anywhere on the planet. This was that rare thing, an idea so simple, so obvious, it was hard to believe no one had thought of it before. Bhatia saw the potential and panicked that someone would steal the idea. He sat up all night writing the business plan. "Then we wrote down all variations of mail—Speedmail, Hypermail, Supermail." Hotmail made perfect sense: it included the letters "html"—the programming language used to write Web pages. A brand name was born.

Bhatia had $6,000 to his name. It was time to find investors. Drive through San Francisco today and every other bill-

board touts some Internet company or other. It was not always like that. . . . "It was a hard story to sell," says Bhatia.
"Few people believed the Net was real. They thought it was a
fad, like CB radio." By the time he reached the offices of venture capitalists Draper Fisher Jurvetson, 19 doors had slammed
behind him. Steve Jurvetson and his colleagues quickly saw
the potential and put up $300,000. Bhatia and Smith stretched
the money all the way to launch day, July 4, 1996. By year-end
they were greeting their millionth customer. When Microsoft
came knocking, 12 months later, they'd signed up nearly 10
million users.

Chronology

1790

First East Indian immigrant appears in Salem, Massachusetts. Identified in colonial records as "man from Madras," he may have been a merchant seaman. Other East Indians came as indentured servants by way of England.

1820

One Indian immigrant is admitted to the United States. From 1820 until 1900, fewer than 700 East Indians migrated to the United States. Most were laborers and agricultural workers. They intermarried with the African American population.

1870s

The American government discourages East Indian immigration to the United States in the post-Civil War period. It argued that Indians were of no value in the settlement of the American West.

1890s

First wave of East Indian immigrants arrives on the west coast of the United States and Canada. Primarily Sikhs from the Punjab, they worked on railroads, in lumber mills, and on farms.

1907

The Asian Exclusion League (AEL) of San Francisco includes East Indians in its plan to keep Asian immigrants out of the United States. The same year, the AEL plays a significant role in the race riot in Bellingham, Washington, in which whites attacked the homes of East Indians and drove the immigrants from the city. East Indian immigration is later suspended by the authorities.

1910

The United States allows East Indians to enter the country to work as laborers on the Western Pacific Railroad.

1913

California enacts the Alien Land Law which restricts anyone ineligible for citizenship to sell or lease land. Indians were ineligible but many found a way around the law by marrying Mexican American women, for whom the law did not apply. The same year Punjabi Indians founded the Ghadar Movement in San Francisco. The movement encouraged East Indians in the United States to return to India to fight for its independence from the British.

1917

The United States Immigration Act declares Asia a "barred zone," thus preventing fresh immigration from Asian countries including India. East Indians in the United States are ineligible for citizenship and cannot own or lease land.

1923

In its decision in the case of Bhagat Singh Thind, the Supreme Court decided that while East Indians were Caucasians in the anthropological sense, they were not white in the common man's understanding of the word and were therefore never intended to be naturalized citizens. The ruling against Thind denied Indians the ability to naturalize and stripped already naturalized Indians of their citizenship.

1924

The U.S. National Origins Act establishes a system of national quotas that practically shut off immigration from Asia.

1930

As a result of discriminatory laws the number of East Indians in the United States drops to 3,130.

1941

The United States enters World War II and looks to India as an ally against Japanese expansionism in Asia. As a result, the government's attitude about Asian immigrants begins to change.

1943

When the United States lifts barriers on Chinese immigration and naturalization Indians argue for the same rights.

1946

The passage of the Luce-Celler bill into law allows East Indians in the United States to become naturalized citizens. East Indians were also given a quota for immigration.

1947

Great Britain grants India independence, an event that heightens American interest in India and its people and culture.

1952

California's Alien Land Law is declared unconstitutional.

1956

Indian-born Dalip Singh Saund is elected to the United States Congress representing California's 29th district. He is the first East Indian elected to office.

1960

There are approximately 50,000 East Indians in the United States.

1965

The United States Immigration Act phases out national origin quotas, thus ending years of discrimination against Asian immigrants.

1968

Asian immigration increases as a result of the United States' new immigration laws. Many immigrants from India arrive in the United States to join family members, pursue education, work in the professions, or flee political persecution.

1970s

There are 70,000 Asian Indians in the United States according to the census. Many live in the borough of Queens in New York City.

1980

The U.S. Census Bureau uses the term Asian Indian for the census to avoid confusion with American Indians and Pakistanis and Bangladeshis.

early 2000s

The East Indian population in the United States numbers over 1.6 million. About 170,900 live in New York City and its suburbs. Other major population centers are Chicago, Los Angeles, Washington, D.C., and San Francisco.

For Further Research

Books

Sripati Chandrasekhar, ed., *From India to America: A Brief History of Immigration; Problems of Discrimination; Admission and Assimilation.* LaJolla, CA: A Population Review Book, 1982.

Colin Clarke, Ceri Peach and Steven Vertovec, eds., *South Asians Overseas: Migration and Ethnicity.* Cambridge, UK: Cambridge University Press, 1990.

Roger Daniels, *Coming to America: A History of Immigration and Ethnicity in American Life.* Second Edition. New York: Perennial, an Imprint of HarperCollins Publishers, 2002.

Sathi S. Dasgupta, *On the Trail of an Uncertain Dream: Indian Immigrant Experience in America.* New York: AMS, Inc., 1989.

Chitra Banerjee Divakaruni, *Arranged Marriages: Stories.* New York: Anchor Books, 1995.

Arthur W. Helweg, *Strangers in a Not-So-Strange Land: Indian American Immigrants in the Global Age.* Belmont, CA: Wadsworth/Thomson, 2004.

Joan M. Jensen, *Passage from India: Asian Indian Immigrants in North America.* New Haven, CT: Yale University Press, 1988.

S. Mitra Kalita, *Suburban Sahibs: Three Immigrant Families and Their Passages from India to America.* New Brunswick, NJ: Rutgers University Press, 2003.

Madhulika S. Khandelwal, *Becoming American, Being Indian: An Immigrant Community in New York City.* Ithaca, NY: Cornell University Press, 2002.

Amitava Kumar, *Away: The Indian Writer as an Expatriate.* New York: Routledge, 2004.

Sunaina Marr Maira, *Desis in the House: East Indian Youth Culture in New York City.* Philadelphia: Temple University Press, 2002.

Sunaina Maira and Rajini Srikanth, eds., *Contours of the Heart: South Asians Map North America.* New York: The Asian American Writers' Workshop, 1996.

Ismail Merchant, *My Passage from India: A Filmmaker's Journey from Bombay to Hollywood and Beyond.* New York: Viking Studio, 2002.

Robert A. Orsi, ed., *Gods of the City: Religion and the American Urban Landscape.* Bloomington: Indiana University Press, 1999.

Padma Rangaswamy, *Namaste America: Indian Immigrants in an American Metropolis.* University Park: The Pennsylvania State University Press, 2004.

David M. Reimers, *Still the Golden Door. The Third World Comes to America.* New York: Columbia University Press, 1992.

Dalip Singh Saund, *Congressman from India.* New York: Dutton, 1960.

Ronald Takaki, *Strangers from a Different Shore: A History of Asian Americans.* Boston: Little Brown, 1998.

Raymond Brady Williams, *Religions of Immigrants from India and Pakistan.* Cambridge, UK: Cambridge University Press, 1988.

Videorecordings

Conquering America, an interview with Bharati Mukherjee. A conversation between Mukherjee and Bill Moyers about America's Asian immigrants and their struggles with learning the new culture (1990).

Mississippi Masala, a film by Mira Nair. The film deals with an East Indian immigrant family who settles in a small Mississippi town, where their daughter falls in love with an African American man (1992).

Roots in the Sand, a PBS documentary by Jayasri Majumdar Hart. The film is about selected multigeneration Punjabi-Mexican families who settled in southern California's Imperial Valley one hundred years ago (2000).

Web Sites

Asian-nation, www.asian-nation.org. A resource and educational center for information on the history, politics, and cultural issues of America's diverse Asian community.

The Asians in America Project, www.asiansinamerica.org. A source of information for all things of interest to people of Asian descent living in the United States. The site provides previously published and original content to community leaders, writers, journalists, educators, students or anyone interested in the Asian American community.

Asian American Net, www.asianamerican.net. A Web site devoted to all Asian American communities. Its goal is to promote and strengthen cultural, educational, and commercial ties between Asia and North America. The site highlights all Asian cultures and Asian Amerians from these cultures. A primary feature is the collection of regional and country-specific materials available on the Internet. For information on South Asia and a list of Indian organizations in America, readers can go to www.asianamerican.net/southasia.html.

Echoes of Freedom: South Asian Pioneers in California, 1899–1965, www.lib.berkeley.edu/SSEAL/echoes/echoes.html. This site presents the story in photographs, documents, and publications of early Indian immigrants to

California. The material is drawn from the exhibit held at the Bernice Layne Brown Gallery, Doe Library, University of California, Berkeley, July 16 to September 30, 2001.

Indian American Center for Political Awareness, www.iacfpa.org. The Web site of IACPA (founded by the publishers of *India Abroad*, the largest circulating Indian American newspaper in the United States) is devoted to increasing awareness in the Indian American community and encouraging the participation by the Indian American community in the American government.

Little India, www.littleindia.com. The online version of *Little India* magazine, the largest circulated Indian publication in the United States. The magazine's focus is the Indian American community. Writers include scholars, professionals, students, artists, and government officials. Articles cover such topics as business, technology, education, lifestyle, and politics.

Index